TRS-80 Interfacing

Book 1

by
Jonathan A. Titus

Howard W. Sams & Co., Inc.
4300 WEST 62ND ST. INDIANAPOLIS, INDIANA 46268 USA

FIRST EDITION
FOURTH PRINTING—1981

International Standard Book Number: 0-672-21633-7
Library of Congress Catalog Card Number: 79-65749

Printed in the United States of America.

Preface

The purpose in writing this book is to introduce you to the signals available within the Radio Shack TRS-80 computer and to show you how they can be used to control external devices, under the control provided by BASIC-language programs. A special design system has been developed to speed your circuit implementation and to allow you to perform easily the many experiments that have been provided. Through the use of a design system, such as the one described later in this book, you will be able to spend your time concentrating on the principles involved, rather than trouble-shooting your circuitry.

As always, in computer systems, input/output (I/O) devices are useless unless they are controlled by computer program steps, or software, that have been written specifically to control them. Unfortunately, the Level I BASIC that is supplied with the TRS-80 in its minimum configuration does not contain any commands that allow I/O devices to be controlled by statements in BASIC programs. The TBUG (Level I) program could be used to allow the entry and execution of *machine language* operation codes in *hexadecimal* format. If you are not familiar with these terms, you can probably understand why we have chosen to avoid their use in this book. We will introduce you to these terms, however, but we will concentrate on the use of BASIC-language programs to control I/O devices.

We have chosen to use the Level II BASIC program, with a minimum of 4K of read/write (R/W) memory available for program and data storage. The Level II BASIC has a number of commands that allow direct communuication with I/O devices, under program control. We will introduce you to these commands shortly. These instructions are easily mastered, without the need for a detailed understanding of the microprocessor chip and the support circuitry contained in the TRS-80 keyboard module.

First we introduce you to the control signals that are available for interfacing and then we start to tell you how they are used. Some of the signals will not be discussed in this book, since they have been provided for use by standard Radio Shack peripherals, and their use is not important to most external I/O devices.

Our next step shows you how the various Level II BASIC instructions are used to control the operation of these signals so that *you* may actually control the flow of data to and from external I/O devices and the computer through BASIC program steps. You will be able to write "low-level" I/O control programs rather quickly. This is one of the beauties of a higher-level or more English-like language, such as BASIC. There are drawbacks to using BASIC for I/O control, as we point out later in the text.

We have assumed that you already have a fairly good understanding of the commands in Level II BASIC. If you are just starting your programming experience with the TRS-80, we hope that you will take some time to become familiar with the basic commands such as INPUT, PRINT, IF, GOTO, FOR, etc. We frequently use these and other program statements in our examples and in the experiments, and we hope that their use will be second-nature after you have finished reading this book.

The last section of the book starts to combine your interfacing and software skills to allow you to understand the power of Level II BASIC as it is applied to the control of external I/O devices. You will also have an opportunity to construct and test a number of interesting interface circuits that will be used in the experiments to reinforce your skills.

We realize that it is often difficult to write a book such as this so that it addresses all audiences, from the beginner to the advanced programmer/hardware designer. We have decided to start someplace near the middle of the spectrum of users. Thus, we have chosen not to review binary numbers, basic digital logic, circuit breadboarding, and other topics. A short review of a paragraph or two will be used, where appropriate, to refresh your knowledge of these areas, but since they have been covered in a great amount of detail elsewhere, we direct you to several references, rather than repeat these subjects here. We will expect that the use of binary numbers and binary/decimal conversions can be performed by you with a minimum of difficulty. We have also assumed some familiarity with the SN7400-series transistor-transistor logic (TTL) family, including such devices as the SN7475 quad latch, the SN7402 quad two-input NOR package, etc.

If you think that some review might be useful, or if these topics or areas are new to you, we suggest the following references.

Breadboarding, microcomputers and digital logic:
Introductory Experiments in Digital Electronics and 8080A Microcomputer Programming and Interfacing (Two volumes, 21550 and 21551).

General microcomputer interfacing and programming:
The 8080A Bugbook®: Microcomputer Interfacing and Programming (21447).

Microcomputer software:
8080/8085 Software Design, Book 1 (21541)
8080/8085 Software Design, Book 2 (21615).

All of the above books are available from Howard W. Sams & Co., Inc., 4300 West 62nd Street, Indianapolis, IN 46206.

The pin configurations for most of the SN 7400-series "chips" are provided through the courtesy of Texas Instruments. Other diagrams and pin configuration figures have been provided by other companies, as noted. The name TRS-80 is a trademark of Radio Shack.

The author thanks Chris and Dave for their proofreading and helpful comments, and Sara Jane Titus for typing the drafts and the final manuscript. I dedicate this book to my own two little "bugs," Chris and Beth.

JONATHAN A. TITUS

Contents

CHAPTER 1

Z-80 Processor 9
 Memory — Input/Output (I/O) Devices — Software I/O Control
 Instructions

CHAPTER 2

TRS-80 Interfacing 27
 I/O Device Address Decoding — Device Addressing

CHAPTER 3

I/O Device Interfacing 47
 Output Ports — Input Ports — Memory-Mapped I/O

CHAPTER 4

Flags and Decisions 61
 I/O Device Synchronization — Logical Operations and Flags —
 Flag-Detecting Software — Complex Flags — Flag Circuits — Multi-
 ple Flags — Interrupts

CHAPTER 5

Breadboarding with the TRS-80 69
 Basic Breadboard

CHAPTER 6

TRS-80 INTERFACE EXPERIMENTS 83
Introduction to the Experiments — Use of the Logic Probe — Use of
the Device Address Decoder — Using Device-Select Pulses — Constructing an Input Port — Multibyte Input Ports — Input-Port Applications — Input-Port Applications (II) — Constructing an Output
Port — Output-Port and Input-Port Interactions — Data Logging
and Display — Simple Digital-to-Analog Converter — Device Address — Decoder Circuits — Output Ports, BCD, and Binary Codes
— Output-Ports Traffic-Light Controller — Logic-Device Tester —
Simple Flag Circuits — Programmable Interface Chips — Interfacing
an Analog-to-Digital Converter

APPENDIX A

LOGIC FUNCTIONS 163

APPENDIX B

PARTS REQUIRED FOR THE EXPERIMENTS 167

APPENDIX C

Z-80 MICROPROCESSOR TECHNICAL DATA 169

APPENDIX D

TRS-80 INTERFACE BREADBOARD PARTS 181

APPENDIX E

PRINTED-CIRCUIT BOARD ARTWORK 183

INDEX 188

1

Z-80 Processor

The Radio Shack TRS-80 computer system uses the Z-80–type of microprocessor integrated circuit. This "chip" forms the heart or central processing unit (CPU) of the computer, the place where the actual mathematical, logical, decision-making, and other operations take place. The Z-80–type microprocessor chip is manufactured by the Zilog Corporation (Cupertino, CA 95014), the Mostek Corporation (Carrollton, TX 75006) as their 3880 chip, and by SGS-Ates (Italy).

The Z-80 chip is an 8-bit processor. Thus, all of the mathematical, logical, data transfer, input, and output operations operate on eight binary bits at a time. Each bit, of course, can be either a logic one or a logic zero. The Z-80 uses an 8-bit data bus to transfer information between itself and various memory locations and input/output (I/O) devices such as a keyboard, printer, etc. In cases where the value of information exceeds the limit of eight bits, multiples of 8-bit data words are used. Each 8-bit data word is generally referred to as a *byte*.

You should realize that the maximum value that can be expressed with eight bits is 11111111_2 or 255_{10}. If larger values are to be operated on in an 8-bit computer system, then multibyte operations are required. Generally, this means that corresponding bytes in two data words are operated on, followed by the operation being performed on the next corresponding set of bytes in the large data words. In this way large values, beyond the value of 255, may be readily processed. It is important to remember, though, that the TRS-80 CPU can only process and transfer eight bits or one byte at a time.

The Z-80 uses a single set of eight pins to make connection with the data bus in the computer. This data bus is used to transfer information both to and from the computer. This type of a bus is called *bidirectional,* since it allows information to flow in two different directions. This is much like a highway that is used to allow vehicles to drive one way in the morning and to allow vehicles to travel in the opposite direction in the evening, perhaps to better accommodate commuter traffic.

The Z-80 generates control signals on the integrated circuit that are used both internally and externally to supervise and manage the flow of information on the bus, in one direction at a time. We will explore the generation and the use of these signals later in this book.

MEMORY

All computer systems have some memory associated with them. In general, the memory is used to store both a program that will control the operation of the computer, as well as the information that is to be processed. In the Z-80–based computer, each memory location can be used to store eight bits of information, or one byte of data. Most memories consist of multiples of these one-byte storage locations, generally in multiples of 1024, abbreviated 1K.

The memory locations must be addressed in some way so that the computer knows exactly where it is to store data or obtain program step information. The Z-80 microprocessor chip has 16 address outputs allowing it to specify any one of 2^{16} or 65,536 memory locations, each of which can contain one byte. This is often shortened to 64K, indicating that 64K *bytes* of information can be addressed. In almost all microcomputer memory systems, each memory location is uniquely addressed with a 16-bit address.

The address bus lines are labeled A0 through A15, corresponding to the least-significant bit (LSB) through the most-significant bit (MSB), respectively. The LSB and MSB can both be either a logic one or a logic zero, but their *position* gives the LSB a *value* of zero or one and the MSB a *value* of zero or $32,768_{10}$. Since the Z-80 is an 8-bit processor, the address lines are frequently split into two groups of eight lines each, A7-A0 and A15-A8. The lines A7-A0 are referred to as the low or LO address, while the lines A15-A8 are referred to as the high or HI address. These lines will be explored further when software instructions are discussed and when interface circuits are developed. Unlike the data bus, the address bus is unidirectional, the address information flows in only one direction, from the CPU to the memory and to external devices.

The pin configuration of the Z-80 is shown in Fig. 1-1. Although most of the other signals will be meaningless to you, you should be

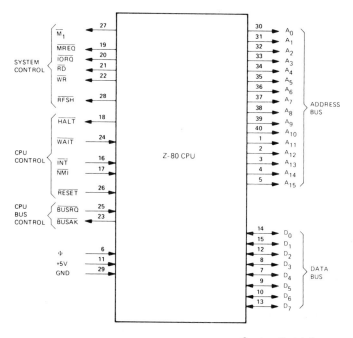

Courtesy Mostek Corp.
Fig. 1-1. Z-80 Microprocessor chip pin configuration.

able to identify the eight data bus input/output pins and the 16 address output pins.

Since the memory section is being discussed, there are several different types of memory devices that are used in microcomputer systems. These are:

Read/Write—Read/Write (R/W) memory is used for the storage of data that will be changed or updated. The computer must be able to place the information in a memory location and then be able to read it back. Programs that will be changed are also stored in R/W memory, for the same reason. The lowest cost TRS-80 contains 4096 or 4K of R/W memory.

Read-Only—Read-only memory (ROM) is used when data values and program steps will not be altered. The BASIC interpreter program in your TRS-80 system is contained in read-only memory chips. The Level II BASIC interpreter is stored in either 12K or 16K of ROM.

There are various sub-classes of these types of memory devices. The R/W memories may be either *static* or *dynamic*. Static memory chips will maintain the values stored in them until they are changed.

Dynamic memories require refreshing by external hardware every few milliseconds or they will "forget" or loose the data stored in them. The R/W memories in the TRS-80 are dynamic, with the necessary refreshing circuitry contained on the computer printed-circuit board.

There are many types of read-only memories. The various types are generally all static, the differences occurring in the means of storing the 8-bit data values in the memory locations. The two most important types are *mask-programmed* and *field-programmed*. The mask-programmed devices have data values, program steps, etc., stored in them during the various manufacturing steps. They are generally referred to as ROMs. The field-programmable devices require some kind of special programming circuitry to store the logic ones and zeros in the various locations. Some of the field-programmable ROMs, or PROMs, as they are generally called, can be erased under high-intensity ultraviolet light. They can then be reprogrammed. This is very useful when programs are being developed that will be stored in read-only memory. It does not require the development of masks and chips, an expensive process, each time a program bug is found or a change is made.

A few final words are required about semiconductor memory devices. The read/write devices are *volatile*, since data (your program and values) will "evaporate" or disappear when power is removed from the system. The read-only memories, on the other hand, are considered to be nonvolatile, since they will maintain the data, or program steps (the Level II BASIC interpreter) when the power has been removed.

Most memory integrated-circuit packages or chips do not have all 16 of the address lines connected to them. They have only enough address connections to uniquely address the memory locations within the individual chip. Thus, a 64-byte chip, small by standards of today, would only have six address line inputs while a 1024 (1K) byte memory chip would have 10 address line inputs. Memory chips such as these have an additional control or chip-enable input that allows banks or groups of the chips to be selected, one set of addresses at a time. Various decoding and selecting circuits may be used, thus allowing a 32K block of memory to be constructed from 64-byte or 1K byte chips, or even combinations of the two. The main point here is that the memory chips do not require all 16 address lines *to be connected directly to them*, although some combination of all 16 address bits will be used to uniquely select one byte. You should not be confused when you are confronted with a 1K $\times$ 4 bit memory that only has 10 address inputs and a chip enable input. This concept will be developed further as you study input/output data transfers.

Two additional control signals are generated by the Z-80 and its support logic. These are READ ($\overline{RD}$) and WRITE ($\overline{WR}$), which control the reading of data from the memory into the Z-80 and the writing of data from the Z-80 to the memory, respectively. In both cases, the Z-80 has specified a 16-bit address to locate the memory "cell" that is to be involved in the transfer. In this case, the cell is an 8-bit word or byte.

The "bar" over the $\overline{RD}$ and $\overline{WR}$ notation indicates that it is a logic zero level that causes the corresponding operation to take place. Thus, $\overline{RD}$ and $\overline{WR}$ are both logic zero pulses, generated by the Z-80 system. The Radio Shack notation for these is RD* and WR*, a nonstandard format that we will not use further. You may also see the notation $\overline{MEMR}$ and $\overline{MEMW}$ for these signals, denoting *memory* read and write operations.

You may also see the notation RAM used to incorrectly signify read/write memory. The acronym RAM stands for *random-access memory*. In fact, all of the modern, easy-to-use memory devices are random access, since one may address one location and then any other, without having to sequence through all of the locations between the two addresses.

Pin configurations for typical memory chips have been provided in Fig. 1-2.

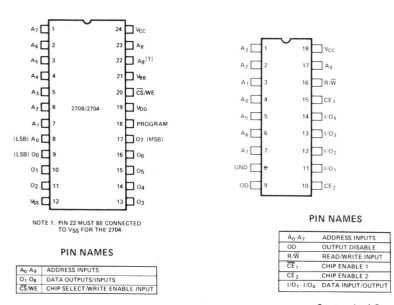

Courtesy Intel Corp.

Fig. 1-2. Pin configurations for 2708 1K × 8-bit PROM and 2111 256 × 4-bit R/W memory chips.

For additional information about memory devices, we refer you to

- *Intel Memory Design Handbook,* Intel Corporation, Santa Clara, CA 95051, 1975.
- *The 8080A/9080A MOS Microprocessor Handbook,* Advanced Micro Devices, Inc., Sunnyvale, CA 94086, 1977.
- *Mostek Memory Products Catalog,* Mostek Corporation, Carrollton, TX 75006, 1977.
- *Bipolar and CMOS Memory Data Book,* Harris Semiconductor Prod. Div., Melbourne, FL 32901, 1978.

INPUT/OUTPUT (I/O) DEVICES

Most microcomputer-based systems are worthless without some attached I/O devices. These devices may be standard peripherals, such as card readers, printers, displays, etc., or they may be sensors, controllers, and other devices that most people do not normally associate with computers. The TRS-80 computer is no exception. It already has three I/O devices associated with it; a television display, a cassette tape recorder, and a keyboard.

Other I/O devices can be added to your computer. These devices may be of your own design or they may be standard, commercially available devices that are compatible with the TRS-80. These I/O devices are much like the individual memory locations that were discussed in the previous section. They are attached to the data bus, since data is transferred to them and from them, and they are also connected to the address bus, although not in exactly the same way as the memory devices. Just as memory locations are uniquely addressed, so are the I/O devices.

Two control signals are provided to synchronize the flow of data to and from I/O devices. These signals are generated by the logic circuits that are associated with the Z-80 chip, and they are called $\overline{\text{IN}}$ and $\overline{\text{OUT}}$. The $\overline{\text{IN}}$ signal controls the flow of data from the I/O devices *to* the Z-80, while the $\overline{\text{OUT}}$ signal controls the flow of data *from* the Z-80 to the I/O devices. As noted previously, the "bar" over the signal name indicates that the logic zero state causes the input or output function to take place. The signals are noted as IN* and OUT* in the Radio Shack manual and you may also see these two signals noted as $\overline{\text{I/OR}}$ and $\overline{\text{I/OW}}$ for I/O-read and I/O-write, respectively. We prefer the $\overline{\text{IN}}$ and $\overline{\text{OUT}}$ notation and we will use it throughout this book.

Since we will be concentrating on the use of I/O devices with the TRS-80, we have left a great deal of the specific discussion to the remaining sections.

Review

At this point, you should understand that the Z-80 transfers and operates on eight bits of data at a time. Complex calculations and operations often require multiple groups of eight bits or bytes. The bytes are transferred to and from the Z-80 CPU on an 8-bit data bus.

The Z-80 uses a 16-bit address bus to address individual memory locations. The 16-bit address bus is broken into a HI and LO address bus, of eight bits each. Input/output devices also use the address bus.

There are four control signals that are used to control the flow of data to and from the CPU and memory, and to and from I/O devices. These signals are active in the logic zero state. The signals and their designations are noted in Table 1-1.

Table 1-1. Control Signals Used for Interfacing

DATA BUS	D7-D0	An 8-bit bidirectional set of lines for transfer of information between the CPU and memory and I/O devices.
ADDRESS BUS	A15-A0	A 16-bit unidirectional address bus used to address both memory and I/O devices
	A15-A8	HI address bus, most-significant eight address bits
	A7-A0	LO address bus, least-significant eight address bits
CONTROL BUS	$\overline{RD}$	Memory read control signal ($\overline{MEMR}$ or RD*)
	$\overline{WR}$	Memory write control signal ($\overline{MEMW}$ or WR*)
	$\overline{IN}$	I/O device input control signal ($I/\overline{OR}$ or IN*)
	$\overline{OUT}$	I/O device output control signal ($I/\overline{OW}$ or OUT*)

NOTES: The "bar" notation, i.e., $\overline{IN}$, indicates a logic zero is the "active" state, the state that causes the corresponding action to take place.

In each case in which a signal is enumerated, the numbers increase as the significance of the bits increases, i.e., A15 = most-significant address bit (MSB).

SOFTWARE I/O CONTROL INSTRUCTIONS

I/O Commands

The TRS-80 computer has a number of instructions that are used to control I/O devices. For the most part, though, these instructions are used to control specific I/O devices or to perform specific functions. Without realizing it, you are already familiar with some, if not all, of these I/O instructions.

Here are some examples of these I/O control instructions, to refresh your memory.

The INPUT and PRINT commands are probably familiar to you. The INPUT command causes a BASIC program to stop and wait for an input from the keyboard. The PRINT command causes an answer or string of characters to be "printed" on the tv screen.

Example 1-1. A Simple I/O Program

```
10  INPUT  "VALUE OF X IS"; X
20  PRINT  "INPUT VALUE WAS"; X
```

If you executed the program in Example 1-1, the value associated with the variable, X, would have to be entered into the computer before the program passed control to statement 20. These two types of I/O statements are frequently used to allow an operator to enter a value and to see a value displayed. There are many variations of both the INPUT and PRINT commands, but these two examples serve to illustrate the point; you have already been using I/O operations in BASIC-language programs without difficulty.

You may have already discovered that there are also *graphic display* I/O commands in BASIC, too. There are the CLS, SET, and RESET commands. The CLS command clears the entire screen, while the SET and RESET commands are used to "turn-on" and "turn-off" rectangular shapes on the tv screen. The SET and RESET commands require the use of "coordinates" to indicate where the operation is to take place.

The program in Example 1-2 shows the use of these three instructions to generate a random display of "on" and "off" locations on the screen. Note that a POINT instruction was used to query the point to determine its current state.

Example 1-2. A Random Pattern Generator using I/O Commands

```
10  CLS
20  X = RND (127)
30  Y = RND (47)
40  IF POINT (X,Y) = 0 GOTO 70
50  RESET (X,Y)
60  GOTO 20
70  SET (X,Y)
80  GOTO 20
```

There are two other commands that you may not have considered to be I/O commands. These are the CLOAD and CSAVE commands that are used to read and store programs on cassette tapes. Each command causes a preset series of operations to take place, controlling the cassette recorder. The use of these commands is fairly obvious, so we will not provide an example.

Other commands are the LPRINT and LLIST operations associated with the optional line printer that can be used with the TRS-80. It is important that you realize that these instructions are all specific to the TRS-80 computer and its BASIC-language interpreter program. These instructions would be meaningless to other Z-80–based computer systems unless they used the TRS-80 Level II BASIC program. The instructions are also specific to one I/O device, i.e., the CLS instruction has no effect on the cassette recorder, *or any other I/O device*. Likewise, the INPUT command controls the input of values only from the keyboard on the console.

General-Purpose I/O Commands

There are no general-purpose I/O commands in the Level I BASIC interpreter. This is the main reason that we have not used it in this writing. The Level II BASIC interpreter contains four general-purpose I/O commands, two of which are used with I/O devices and two of which are used to examine and change the content of memory locations.

The two I/O device commands are OUT and INP. They are used to transfer data to an external device from the computer, and to the computer from an external device. There is a specific format for these instructions that must be used if the instructions are to operate properly.

The output instruction, OUT, must specify the *address* of the I/O device that is to be involved in the transfer of data and also the value that is to be transferred to the addressed device. The actual format for the OUT instructions is, OUT x,y, where the x value represents the *decimal* address of the output device that is to receive the data value, y. The data, y, must also be a decimal number. The address and the data value must both be within the range of 0 to 255, inclusive. This means that data values between these limits may be sent to any of up to 256 output devices. The limit on the upper value of a number that can be output should be quickly associated with the largest number that can be transferred on an 8-bit data bus, 255. Remember that there are actually 256 values that can be represented, since zero is a value, too. The limit of 256 output devices (ports) may not be so quickly apparent. We will discuss this further in a later section.

In the following statement, the value 125 is sent to output port 12; OUT 12, 125.

The input instruction, INP, is similar to the OUT instruction, except that no data value is incorporated in the command. We are interested in determining the value present at the specific input device, so only the decimal address of the input device is specified; INP (x), where x is the decimal address of the input device.

It does little good to input a value without doing something with it, so the input command is always incorporated in a complete statement, rather than being a statement itself. An example of this is A = INP(19).

In this case, the variable, A, is assigned the decimal value that has been input from input device 19. It is important that you remember to enclose the address of the device in parentheses.

Whenever an input command, INP, is used, the value that is input will be between zero and 255, inclusive. Again, this is due to the limitation of 8-bit data transfers. Input and output devices will be referred to as *ports*. Thus an output device will be an *output port* and an input device will be an *input port*. This is standard nomenclature used throughout the microcomputer industry.

The input and output commands may have variables specified within them, rather than specific values for port addresses, and in the case of the output instruction, data values. Thus, all of the input and output commands shown in Table 1-2 are valid. We have assumed, of course, that the values for the variables N, M, X, and Q have been specified somewhere in the program prior to the use of the instructions shown in Table 1-2.

Table 1-2. Valid INPUT (INP) and OUTPUT (OUT) Command Structures

OUT 12, 15	INP (15)
OUT N, 120	INP (Q)
OUT 12, X	
OUT X, M	

Input and output commands in which either the data or address values exceed 255 result in an error condition, FC (Illegal Function Call).

We have provided some examples that show the use of the INP and OUT statements. While the program shown in Example 1-3 can be executed, they will not do anything useful, since you do not have any external I/O ports connected to your computer, at present.

Example 1-3. Simple I/O Programs for INP and OUT Commands

```
10   INPUT "OUTPUT PORT # ="; P
20   INPUT "VALUE FOR OUTPUT"; V
30   OUT P,V
40   GOTO 10

10   INPUT "INPUT PORT # ="; I
20   PRINT "VALUE AT PORT ="; INP (I)
30   GOTO 10
```

There are two I/O ports that are used in the TRS-80 itself. Output port 255 controls the cassette recorder and a video display function, while input port 255 is used to input data from the cassette to the computer. The program shown in Example 1-4 allows you to exercise output port 255. You may wish to try this program on your TRS-80 system.

Example 1-4. A Simple Control Program for Port 255

```
10   INPUT "VALUE"; V
20   OUT 255,V
30   FOR I = 1 TO 500: NEXT I
```

```
40   OUT 255, 0
50   FOR I = 1 TO 500: NEXT I
60   GOTO 20
```

If you use the program in Example 1-4, we suggest that you try VALUES that are powers of two: 1, 2, 4, 8, etc. This will allow you to test the effects of different bits. For example, $2_{10} = 00000010_2$ and $8_{10} = 00001000_2$.

You will notice that the value 8 affects the display of the data, while the value 4 controls the cassette recorder. The program operations at lines 30 and 50 provide time delays, so that the action at the port may be observed. You will be able to hear the small cassette tape control relay "buzz" if you change the time delay in lines 30 and 50 from 500 to 5, using the value 4 at output port 255.

You will see later in this book that the INP and OUT instructions can be very powerful.

General-Purpose Memory Commands

There are two general-purpose memory commands in Level II BASIC that also provide a great deal of flexibility in handling some programming tasks. These two commands allow the content of a specific 8-bit memory location to be examined (displayed), and they also allow a value to be stored in a specific memory location. The values that may be stored and retrieved from a memory location are again limited to 8-bit numbers, so only values between 0 and 255 may be used.

The PEEK command allows you to examine the content of any of the possible 64K memory locations of the TRS-80. The decimal address of the location must be specified as a part of the PEEK instruction. The PEEK instruction is used with other instructions to form a complete statement:

PRINT PEEK (200)   or   A = PEEK (5000)

A similar memory-access instruction, POKE, allows a decimal value to be placed in a specific location. As was the case for the PEEK instruction, a decimal address must be specified along with the decimal value that is to be stored:

POKE X,Y

where x is the decimal address of the location and where y is the value to be stored. Thus the statement:

POKE 20000, 10

could be used to store the value 10 in location 20,000. The PEEK command could be used to examine the location to be sure the value 10 was actually stored there:

You must be careful when you use the POKE command, since its careless use may cause information to be stored "on top of" some of your BASIC-language program steps, wiping out your program. *You cannot POKE values into read-only memory.*

Although the Z-80 chip, and the TRS-80, can actually address 64K (65,536) different memory addresses, the PEEK and POKE commands can not directly address locations that are in the upper half of the memory, that is, locations between addresses 32,768 and 65,536, inclusive. This does not mean that these locations are inaccessible, but rather that a different addressing mode must be used to access them. When the address to be used in the PEEK or POKE command is greater than 32,767, the following formula must be used:

$$\text{ADDRESS} = -1*(\text{DESIRED ADDR} - 32767)$$

The program shown in Example 1-5 illustrates the use of the PEEK command to display the decimal content of every 256th memory location. If the address is larger than 32,767, the formula for the address calculation is used. This limit on the values used for the address portion of the PEEK and POKE commands is a function of the mathematical and addressing capabilities of the TRS-80 computer.

Example 1-5. Memory Dump Program To Examine Every 256th Memory Location

```
 10   FOR I = 0 TO 65536   STEP 256
 15   M = I
 20   IF I > 32767 THEN GOTO 100
 30   PRINT I; "      "; PEEK (M)
 40   NEXT I
 50   END
100   M = -1*(I - 32767)
110   GOTO 30
```

You should now be able to see how the PEEK and POKE commands may be used to store and retrieve data values in the TRS-80 read/write memory. At this point, you may be concerned that the INP, OUT, PEEK and POKE commands can transfer only eight bits (decimal 0-255) of information or data. It is not difficult to see a limitation in this. We will shortly explore the transfer of large numbers and data that require 10 or even 12 bits of resolution.

Software Commands and Interface Circuits

As you are probably aware by now, the INP, OUT, PEEK and POKE instructions all cause some actions to take place, either at I/O devices or at memory locations, as a direct result of the use of the instruction. Instructions such as $A = 1.359$ will cause some values to be stored in memory, but we do not know what memory locations the TRS-80 has assigned to the variable "A" and we do not know how the value 1.359 is stored. The INP, OUT, PEEK and POKE instructions all cause a definite, known sequence of operations to take place, transferring data bytes, generating control signals, and transferring address information on the address-bus lines. These definite and reproducible actions allow us to use these commands to control I/O devices. We will now explore the actions that each of these four software commands cause to take place.

The INP and OUT commands operate in a very similar manner. In each, an address is specified, requiring eight bits of information. During the execution of either instruction, the *address* information contained within the command is transferred to external devices on the *LO address bus*, address lines A7-A0. In this way, the I/O device address is available to all of the circuits and devices that are connected to these address lines, both memory and I/O devices.

When an OUT instruction is used in a program, the data value is also output by the Z-80 chip, but on the data-bus lines, D7-D0. Once the data bits, and the LO address bits are "stable" or present on their respective buses in useable form, the Z-80 asserts the $\overline{\text{OUT}}$ signal on the control bus. This synchronizes the acquisition of the data by the I/O device that was addressed. Of course, external circuitry is required to "capture" the data, as well as to identify the selected I/O device and synchronize it with the Z-80–based system. A timing diagram for these signals, as they appear on the Z-80 system, in this case the TRS-80, is shown in Fig. 1-3. At this point, we are only concerned with what the Z-80 does during an OUT command.

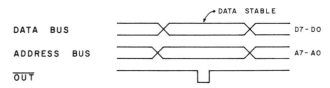

Fig. 1-3. OUT command timing relationships.

When an INP instruction is executed, the data is not contained in the instruction, but is acquired from an external I/O device. Only the address is specified. The address is placed on the LO address-bus lines when the INP instruction is executed. When the address information is present, the Z-80 generates an IN synchronizing pulse that indicates to the addressed I/O device that it is to place its data on the eight data-bus lines when IN is a logic zero.

Additional circuitry is required here, too, to select the I/O device and to gate its data onto the data bus. In this case, the data flow from the I/O device to the computer. A typical timing diagram for an INP command execution is shown in Fig. 1-4.

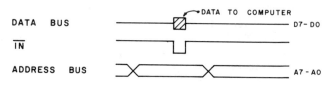

Fig. 1-4. INP command timing relationships.

We will describe shortly some of the circuits that are used for input and output devices. You have probably realized that while we have described an *I/O port* as one that can either receive data that is output by the microcomputer or transmit data that is input by the microcomputer, some *I/O devices* may actually contain a number of I/O ports. Industrial controllers, data storage devices, (discs, cassettes), analog converters and other I/O devices may have a number of input and output ports, since they may require more than eight bits of information from the computer and they may also need to transfer more than eight bits of data to the computer. In any case, transfers of data that contain more than eight bits always involve the transfer of multiple bytes to and from the individual 8-bit I/O ports. This is important to remember: *data are always transferred eight bits at a time.*

PEEK and POKE Instructions and Interface Circuits

The PEEK and POKE instructions operate in a manner that is similar to the INP and OUT instructions. The main differences between these two sets of instructions are the use of different control or synchronizing signals ($\overline{RD}$ and $\overline{WR}$ instead of $\overline{IN}$ and $\overline{OUT}$) and the use of the entire 16-bit address bus.

Since the PEEK and POKE commands are used to address memory locations, the entire 16-bit address bus must be used to allow any of the 64K possible memory locations to be accessed. (Remember the address "calculation" formula). Thus, during the execution of these two commands, the specified address is output on the 16-bit address bus. When the INP and OUT commands are executed, only the LO address portion (eight bits) of the address bus is used. When the PEEK command is used to determine the content of a memory location, the memory location is addressed by the decimal address value contained in the PEEK command. However, when the PEEK command is executed, the 16-bit binary equivalent of the specified decimal address is actually placed on the address bus by the Z-80. The Z-80 generates a memory read signal, $\overline{RD}$, once the 16-bit memory address has been specified to synchronize the actual data transfer process so that the data flow from the memory to the Z-80 in an orderly fashion.

Likewise, the POKE command specifies an address that is represented by 16 bits. This instruction also specifies the 8-bit value, in decimal form, that is to be written into the desired location. When the POKE command is executed, the 16-bit address is output on the address bus, along with the 8-bit data value on the data bus. The Z-80 also generates a memory write pulse, $\overline{WR}$, to synchronize the actual acquisition of the data by the R/W memory chips from the data bus.

A combined timing diagram for the PEEK and POKE commands is shown in Fig. 1-5. You should note the similarity between the timing information in this figure and that in Figs. 1-3 and 1-4.

You must remember that even though not all of the 64K possible memory locations may be used or available in your computer, a unique 16-bit address has been assigned to each location. Thus, you must always specify a unique 16-bit address to point to a specific address when the PEEK and POKE instructions are used. Likewise, while not all 256 possible I/O devices will be connected to your system, each I/O device must be identified through the use of a complete 8-bit device address when the INP and OUT instructions are used.

Software Commands—Data Transfer and Control

In most cases, the four general-purpose I/O software commands, INP, OUT, PEEK and POKE, will be used to transfer 8-bit data values between the I/O devices or memory locations and the Z-80 computer. As we noted previously, some data transfers will require more than eight bits of information, so multiple bytes are transferred, one byte at a time.

There are also cases in which the actual *value* of the data transferred is meaningless. The bits may be used to represent individual two-state conditions that are unrelated to the positional values of the bits. For example, a number of sensors may be connected to the TRS-80 indicating conditions such as tank empty or full, heater on or off, valve open or closed, and so on. An INP command could be used to input the status of these bits, through an 8-bit input port. Thus, the value read from this input port might be 100, but the port is *sensing* eight individual on or off (logic one or logic zero) states, so the value of 100_{10} is meaningless. The individual binary bits each represent the state of an individual sensor. In this case:

$$100_{10} = 01100100_2$$

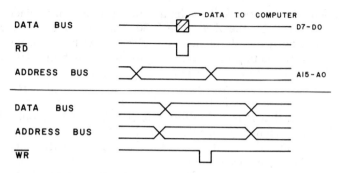

Fig. 1-5. PEEK and POKE command timing relationships.

This indicates that three sensors are in the logic one state and five are in the logic zero state.

The OUT instruction can be used in a similar manner to turn a device on or to turn a device off, based on the state of individual bits. You have already seen this, in Example 1-4.

It is important to keep in mind the use of I/O ports. Either data or control information may be transferred between these I/O devices and the computer. We will explore this more in later sections in which actual control circuits are developed. Both the data and control modes will be used. The actual use of the INP and OUT instructions are not affected by the mode of operation or the use to which the information is put. The computer does not care whether the *value* 210 is being output or whether the binary bit pattern 11010010 is being output to a control device.

Assembly Language and BASIC

The BASIC language programs that you write on your TRS-80 system bear very little relationship to the actual instructions that the Z-80 microprocessor chip can actually execute. Each of your BASIC statements and commands is *interpreted* by the BASIC *interpreter* resident within the TRS-80 system. A programming manual for the Z-80 chip, itself, would bear little relationship to the Level II BASIC manual. The commands are very different.

The Z-80 chip does not have a PRINT command, so it could not perform the following operation:

PRINT "THIS IS A TEST"

The BASIC interpreter determines that a PRINT operation is to take place and it then executes a series of assembly language program instructions that actually place the codes for the alphabetical characters in the display memory to spell-out, "THIS IS A TEST." The assembly language steps consist of logic ones and zeros that cause the necessary internal and external Z-80 operations to take place to transfer the message portion of the PRINT command to the display memory.

While we will not require you to learn and use the Z-80 assembly language in this book, you should be aware that it is the "base" computer language that causes the actual operations to take place.

The INP, OUT, PEEK, and POKE commands each cause many, many assembly language statements to be executed to produce the overall effect of data transfer. Since these BASIC language instructions must be interpreted, even when used one right after another, or in a loop, the *interpretation* software process can be slow. Two programs are shown in Example 1-6, an assembly language output program and a BASIC-language output program. Each accomplishes the same task, the transfer of a data byte to an output port. The programs are not particularly useful, but they do allow a simple comparison to be made in the speed of execution.

Example 1-6. Comparison of Assembly Language and BASIC Programs for Data Output

BASIC PROGRAM	ASSEMBLY LANGUAGE
10 P=100	MVI A
20 D=255	FF
30 OUT P,D	LOOP, OUT
40 GOTO 30	64
	JMP
	LOOP
	0

Since each program generates a series of pulses on the $\overline{\text{OUT}}$ control line, the time between the occurrence of these pulses is an indication of the processing speed of each program. The BASIC program can output a data word every 6 milliseconds, while an equivalent assembly language program takes *12 microseconds*. In this example, the assembly language test program is 500 times faster than the BASIC program. We must admit, though, that many other factors must be considered when choosing between programming languages. In fact, assembly language programming is generally not recommended for the novice.

We will mention assembly language programming very little, concentrating on the use of the BASIC language instead. For further information on Z-80 assembly language programming, we recommend *Z-80 Microprocessor Programming and Interfacing* and *The Z-80 Microcomputer Handbook* (Howard W. Sams & Co., Inc., Indianapolis, IN 46268).

Binary and Decimal Numbering

The TRS-80 computer system acquires, processes and prints decimal (base-10) numbers. This makes it compatible with the numbering used by most people today. It would be difficult for us to readily understand and convert data values that were printed in a non-decimal format. The data and address lines are directly connected to the Z-80 chip, so they are binary, having only two states, a logic one or a logic zero. Thus, when we specify an I/O device address in an INP or OUT command, we must realize that the address (0-255) will appear in its binary form on the address bus (00000000_2-11111111_2). You should be able to make the conversion between binary and decimal, in either direction.

Likewise, the data values transferred to and from the computer by INP, OUT, PEEK, and POKE commands are also specified or acquired as 8-bit binary values, since the data bus is only eight bits "wide." This 8-bit data bus is a function of the data processing capability within the Z-8 chip. It is *not* a function of the TRS-80. Thus, we are limited to 8-bit data transfers. Is this a great limitation? Generally not. In spite of it, the TRS-80 can process a great deal of information, and, as you will see, it is easy to interface to I/O devices.

2

TRS-80 Interfacing

At this point, you are probably wondering:

- How does the TRS-80 actually transfer information to I/O devices?
- How are the I/O devices actually synchronized to the operation of the computer?
- How are individual I/O devices selected and identified?
- How do I/O devices place their data on the data bus and how do they actually receive it from the data bus?

These are important questions, since the answers to them will provide the basis for your understanding of microcomputer interfacing. We will be answering these questions in this chapter and we will also provide some experiments that will reinforce the concepts through hands-on experience.

In this chapter, some examples of digital circuits will be provided. We have assumed that you can "read" and interpret a logic circuit diagram, and that you are familiar with the more common SN7400-series transistor-transistor logic (TTL) circuits.

I/O DEVICE ADDRESS DECODING

Before we can discuss the actual transfer of information between I/O devices and the computer, we must first understand the circuitry and the signals that are used to identify or address the individual I/O devices. There are many schemes that may be used, and we will examine several of them. It is impossible to show every possible scheme for addressing I/O devices, since modifications will be made to suit special needs.

When the TRS-80 computer is programmed to perform a data transfer using any of the four general-purpose I/O commands PEEK, POKE, INP or OUT, certain signals are generated by the Z-80 to synchronize the flow of data. At this point, our main concern is the use of the address-bus lines. These are the lines that address individual memory locations and they are also used to address I/O devices.

You should recall that the INP and OUT instructions both contained decimal address information that is used to identify the addressed I/O device. Likewise, the PEEK and POKE instructions also contained decimal address information that is used to identify one of the 64K possible memory locations. The PEEK and POKE instructions have a larger range of addresses that may be specified. The information in Table 2-1 summarizes the address relationships between these four instructions.

Table 2-1. Address Relationships for the Four General-Purpose I/O Commands

Command	Address Limits	Address Bus Use
INP, OUT	0 - 255	A7 - A0
PEEK, POKE	0 - 65,536*	A15 - A8 and A7 - A0

* May require address "calculation."

As shown in Table 2-1, the I/O control instructions INP and OUT only use the LO address bus, A7-A0, for device addressing. This is reasonable, since these eight address lines would limit the address to 00000000_2 to 11111111_2 or 0_{10} to 255_{10}. Thus, each I/O device must be capable of recognizing its own I/O address on the LO address bus. To differentiate between the addressing of I/O devices with the INP and OUT commands, and the addressing of memory locations by the PEEK and POKE commands, we will refer to the INP and OUT command addressing as *device addressing* and to the PEEK and POKE command addressing as *memory addressing*.

DEVICE ADDRESSING

Each I/O device that is to be used with the computer must be able to recognize its own device address. Since the INP and OUT commands use 8-bit addresses, each I/O device must monitor these eight address lines, A7-A0, for the occurrence of its address. There are three basic schemes that may be used by I/O device circuits to accomplish the monitoring for specific addresses. These are:

- *Gating*—detecting a specific combination of logic signals.

- *Decoding*—a more flexible gating scheme in which many addresses may be detected.
- *Comparing*—comparing a preset or known address with the address-bus signals until a match occurs.

Combinations of these three techniques are possible and there are probably many variations that are possible. We will describe examples of each of the three basic decoding schemes.

Using Gates for Address Decoding

In the scheme for decoding device addresses in which individual gates are used, the address must be known so that the gates can be properly configured. In this example, we will use the device address 01111011_2 or 123_{10}. Since NAND/AND gates are the predominant type of gating logic available, we will use these types of circuits in our logic. To refresh your memory, the pin configurations for several types of NAND/AND gates are shown in Fig. 2-1, with the

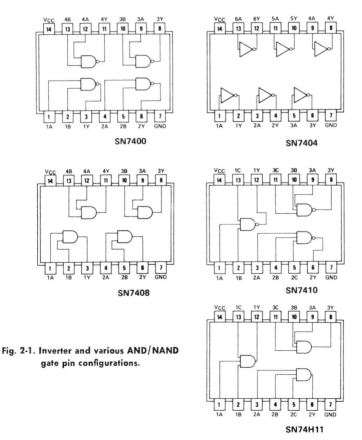

SN7400

SN7404

SN7408

SN7410

Fig. 2-1. Inverter and various AND/NAND gate pin configurations.

SN74H11

29

generalized truth table for a two-input AND gate and an equivalent NAND gate shown in Table 2-2. Since inverters such as the SN7404, are often found in device addressing circuits, a pin configuration for this chip has been included in Fig. 2-1. The truth tables in Table 2-2 also show the function of an inverter.

Table 2-2. Truth Tables for a Two-Input AND Gate, NAND Gate
and an Inverter

AND Gate		NAND Gate		Inverter	
Inputs A B	Output Q	Inputs A B	Output Q	Input A	Output Q
0 0	0	0 0	1	0	1
0 1	0	0 1	1	1	0
1 0	0	1 0	1		
1 1	1	1 1	0		

In all cases, the logic one state is the higher voltage (+2.8 to +5 volts) and the logic zero state is the lower voltage (0.0 to 0.8 volt). The NAND gate devices are available with 2, 3, 4, 8, and 13 inputs, while the AND gates are available with 2, 3, or 4 inputs.

Since the unique output state, logic one for an AND gate and logic zero for a NAND gate occurs only when *all* of the inputs to an AND or a NAND gate are all logic ones, we will have to configure the address 01111011_2 so that it generates eight logic ones at the inputs to an eight input NAND gate when it is present on address lines A7-A0. This simply means that the logic zeros at positions D7 and D2 must be inverted, as shown in Fig. 2-2.

The output of the SN7430 NAND gate will be a logic zero *only* when *all of the inputs are logic one.* Thus, only address 01111011_2 will cause the NAND gate output to go to a logic zero. If a logic

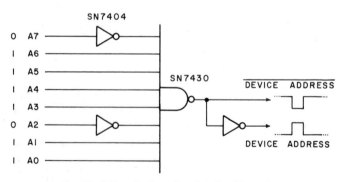

Fig. 2-2. Gating circuit used to decode address 123.

one is required by the I/O device when this address is present, it is obtained by simply inverting the NAND gate output, as shown. The inverters are SN7404 devices. The outputs are labeled $\overline{\text{DEVICE ADDRESS}}$ and DEVICE ADDRESS, respectively, to indicate the logic state that is unique, or that will be used to cause the action to take place at the I/O device.

While this gating scheme is effective in decoding a single address, and relatively inexpensive, it is inflexible. A more flexible scheme is shown in Fig. 2-3. This circuit illustrates the use of a

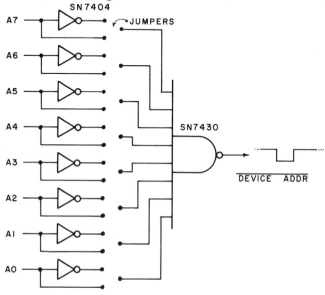

Fig. 2-3. Programmable gating circuit used for device address decoding.

gating scheme in which inverters may be used to invert individual address bits, as required. The bits may also be used without any inversion. The eight jumpers allow the device address to be preset, as illustrated in Fig. 2-4, for address 150, or 10010110_2. If the programmable circuit shown in Fig. 2-3 is used to "detect" the device address, any one of the 256 possible addresses may be preset. Only one address may be preset at one time.

The programmable gating circuit provides broad flexibility, but it can only detect *one* of 256 possible addresses. This is a limitation, particularly when a number of I/O devices are located on the same circuit board; each will require its own gating circuit. We will see shortly how this limitation can be overcome.

Unfortunately, the gating schemes that we have shown will not uniquely identify an address of the I/O device. The address bus

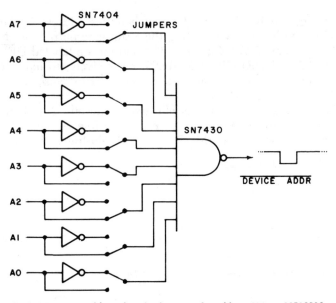

Fig. 2-4. Programmable gating circuit, preset for address 150, or 10010110_2.

is also used to address memory locations, so there is an excellent chance that the 8-bit address of the I/O device will be present on the address bus at other times, not as an I/O device address, *but as the LO address portion of a 16-bit memory address.* Thus, the following 16-bit addresses, 00000000 01111011, 10101111 01111011 and 00110100 01111011, would *all* activate the device address detecting circuit shown in Fig. 2-2. Obviously, there must be some additional circuitry that can be used to allow us to have the device address circuit differentiate between I/O device addresses and memory addresses that are present on the 16-bit address bus.

The information in Table 2-3 shows the relationships between the INP, OUT, PEEK, and POKE instructions. (Memory transfers that are performed by a BASIC program, without the use of the PEEK and POKE commands, are still equivalent to the PEEK and POKE operations in their generation of address and control signals.)

Table 2-3. Relationship of I/O Commands and the Control Signals

Command	Data Bus	Address Bus	Control Signals			
			$\overline{WR}$	$\overline{RD}$	$\overline{IN}$	$\overline{OUT}$
INP	I/O → Z80	A7 - A0	1	1	0	1
OUT	I/O ← Z80	A7 - A0	1	1	1	0
PEEK	MEM → Z80	A15-A8 & A7-A0	1	0	1	1
POKE	MEM ← Z80	A15-A8 & A7-A0	0	1	1	1

As shown, the $\overline{\text{IN}}$ and $\overline{\text{OUT}}$ signals must be used by the I/O device address gating circuit to indicate that the address present on the LO address bus is an I/O device and not a memory address. In most cases, the $\overline{\text{IN}}$ or $\overline{\text{OUT}}$ signal is gated with the output of the 8-input address-detecting NAND gate, as shown in Fig. 2-5.

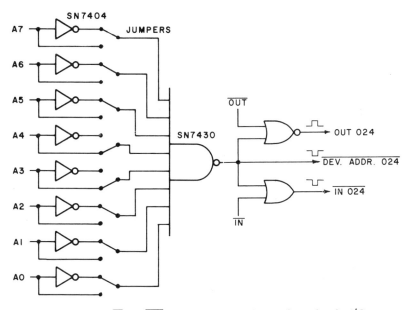

Fig. 2-5. Using $\overline{\text{IN}}$ and $\overline{\text{OUT}}$ signals to generate device select pulses for I/O device synchronization.

Note that a NOR gate and an OR gate have been used to combine the logic-zero $\overline{\text{OUT}}$ and $\overline{\text{IN}}$ signals with the logic-zero output of the device address detecting gate. By way of review, the truth tables for an OR gate and for a NOR gate are provided in Table 2-4. Pin configurations for an SN7432 OR gate and an SN7402 NOR gate integrated circuit are shown in Fig. 2-6.

Table 2-4. Truth Tables for a Two-Input NOR Gate and OR Gate

NOR Gate			OR Gate		
Inputs		Output	Inputs		Output
A	B	Q	A	B	Q
0	0	1	0	0	0
0	1	0	0	1	1
1	0	0	1	0	1
1	1	0	1	1	1

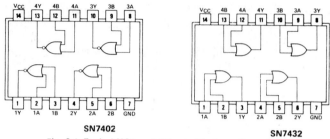

Fig. 2-6. Typical NOR and OR gate IC pin configurations.

The gating scheme now has two "qualified" outputs, one generated through the combination of the $\overline{\text{IN}}$ and the "$\overline{\text{DEVICE AD-DRESS}}$" signals, and the other generated through the combination of the $\overline{\text{OUT}}$ and the "DEVICE ADDRESS" signals. The resulting pulse from each gate is called a *device select pulse,* since it can actually be used to select an input device or an output device. The *only* combination of signals that will generate the device select signals $\overline{\text{OUT 024}}$ or $\overline{\text{IN 024}}$ is the proper 8-bit device address, generated by the address gating, *and* the proper qualifying *function pulse,* $\overline{\text{OUT}}$ or $\overline{\text{IN}}$, respectively. Since this combination of signals is generated only when the computer performs an I/O operation, they indicate that the address on the LO address bus is an I/O device address. Since memory transfers do not and cannot generate these pulses, $\overline{\text{IN}}$ and $\overline{\text{OUT}}$, there is no chance that devices IN 024 or OUT 024 will be selected, even when the *address detecting gate* indicates that address 024 is on the LO address bus, probably indicating the LO portion of a 16-bit memory address.

In all cases, devices will be selected through the use of a *device address* and a *function pulse* to generate a *device select* signal.

The circuit shown in Fig. 2-5 generates a device select for both an input device and an output device with the same I/O device address, address 024. Is this possible? It is, since an input and an output operation cannot be performed at the same time and, thus, the $\overline{\text{IN}}$ and $\overline{\text{OUT}}$ pulses cannot be coincident. The same *device address* may be used with an input device and an output device. The devices may, or may not, be related, or even close to one another. Two or more input or output devices are *not* assigned the same device address, so that you would not have two devices OUT 27 and OUT 27 in a system. The concepts and circuits developed in this section are very important and they will be carried forward to other sections. It is important that you understand the use of the signals that have been discussed to select devices. We have not yet discussed what these input and output devices are, or how they operate, but we shall discuss this shortly.

Using Decoders

In many cases, it is easier to use *decoder* circuits in place of the NAND-gate address detecting circuits, and, in some cases, in place of the NOR-gate device select circuits, too. Why are decoders so useful? Perhaps it is best to take a look at several types of decoders to see what they look like and how they operate. As you examine the decoder circuits, keep in mind that they are simply collections of gates that have been "integrated" into an easy-to-use decoder circuit.

Decoder circuits are generally specified as *x-line to y-line* decoders, where x represents the number of binary inputs, say four inputs, and where y represents the number of possible outputs, or the number of different binary states present on the x input. Thus, for the four inputs, there would be 16 possible outputs, creating a 4-line to 16-line decoder or a 4- to 16-line decoder. This is, in fact, a real circuit, as you will see.

Each of the binary inputs has two states, a logic one and a logic zero. These inputs are all independent of one another. The outputs are also binary, in the sense that they have two possible values, but they are *not independent*. There will only be *one* unique output from the decoder, representing the value or "weight" present at the binary inputs. In most cases, the unique output state is a logic zero, with the other outputs in their logic one state.

A typical decoder integrated circuit is the SN74LS139. This integrated circuit actually contains two independent two-line to four-line decoders, as shown in Fig. 2-7.

The truth table for the SN74LS139 decoder is shown in Table 2-5.

Of course, the truth table applies to both of the decoders within the SN74LS139 integrated-circuit package, or "chip." Most decoder

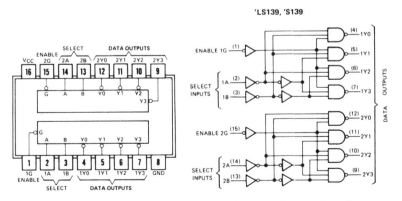

Fig. 2-7. SN74LS139 decoder chip schematic diagram and pin configuration.

Table 2-5. Truth Table for an SN74LS139 Decoder

Inputs			Outputs			
Enable G	Select B	A	Y0	Y1	Y2	Y3
H	X	X	H	H	H	H
L	L	L	L	H	H	H
L	L	H	H	L	H	H
L	H	L	H	H	L	H
L	H	H	H	H	H	L

H = high level   L = low level   X = irrelevant (don't care)

circuits incorporate an enabling input, so that the decoder may be turned on or turned off by one logic input. This is the function of ENABLE or "G" input on each of the decoders in the SN74LS139. Note that when the "G" input is a logic one, all of the outputs are forced into the logic one state, regardless of the states of the A and B inputs. This allows the decoder to be gated on or off. In the off state, the power is not removed, but the outputs are all forced into the logic one state.

Let us now examine a simple, and rather trivial, example of the use of a two-line to four-line decoder for device address decoding. We will assume that we only have a few I/O devices, so that the decoders in the SN74LS139 decoder package can handle our needs. A typical decoder circuit is shown in Fig. 2-8. In this circuit, only

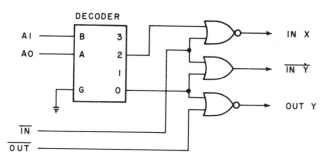

Fig. 2-8. Two-line to four-line decoder used for device addressing.

two address bits have been decoded, the rest have been ignored. Note that the enable input has been grounded so that the outputs of the decoder operate properly. The added NOR and OR gates generate the actual device select pulses.

The device select signals have been noted as IN X, IN Y, and OUT Y, since there is no *specific* address that will actuate each. Device addresses 00000010, 11110110 and 11111010 will all cause the IN X device select pulse to be generated, if they are used in

INP commands, for example A = INP(2), A = INP(246), or A = INP(250). This *nonabsolute* device addressing results because address bits A7-A2 have not been used in the decoding scheme. Nonabsolute addressing means that there are several addresses that will actuate the selected device. The circuit shown in Fig. 2-8 will decode four addresses and thus eight individual devices may be selected, four input devices and four output devices. Additional NOR gates or OR gates are required, though. In a small system, this may be adequate, although the decoding scheme does not provide a great deal of flexibility in allowing the addition of new I/O devices, beyond the eight original ones. Even though this scheme is not very flexible, let's take a closer look at it since it will allow us to develop two other concepts that can be applied to other decoder schemes.

In Fig. 2-8, the enable input, "G," of the decoder is simply grounded, to always enable the decoding action. This input can allow the decoder to be used for *absolute* decoding. A six-input NAND gate circuit can be used to supply an enabling signal to the decoder only when a preset pattern of address bits, on address lines A7-A2, is present. You have already seen the use of the 8-input NAND gate address decoding approach, and the decoder/NAND-gate circuit shown in Fig. 2-9 is a combination of two address selection techniques.

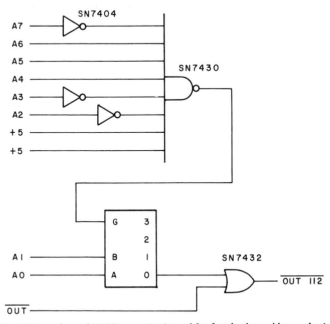

Fig. 2-9. Decoder and NAND-gate circuit used for for absolute address selection.

In this example (Fig. 2-9), the decoder is only enabled when the A7-A2 address bit pattern is 011100, the decoder being used to then decode address bits A0 and A1. In this circuit then, the decoder outputs 0, 1, 2 and 3 correspond to device addresses 112, 113, 114 and 115, respectively (binary 01110000, 01110001, 01110010 and 01110011). Only the $\overline{\text{OUT 112}}$ device select pulse has been generated in this example. Again, an OR gate or a NOR gate is required for each device select signal that is to be generated.

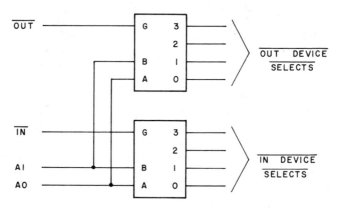

Fig. 2-10. Decoder enable inputs used with $\overline{\text{IN}}$ and $\overline{\text{OUT}}$ to generate device select signals.

An alternate approach is to use both of the decoder circuits in the SN74LS139 "chip," using the $\overline{\text{IN}}$ and $\overline{\text{OUT}}$ function pulses to enable the decoders. In this way, the address selection is again *nonabsolute*, but the device select gating is performed within the chip. This is shown in Fig. 2-10. The NOR and OR gates are no longer required for each device select pulse to be generated.

While this circuit may not be particularly useful, it illustrates the use of the enable input of the decoder to generate the device select pulses. The decoder gating or enabling input may be used for device select pulse generation, or for absolute decoding. In some cases, it may be used for both.

Larger Decoders

There are additional decoder circuits that will be useful to you in interfacing your TRS-80 computer to external devices. These decoders, depending on the type you choose, may have additional inputs, enable lines and outputs. Examples are shown in Fig. 2-11 for the SN74LS138 decoder and in Fig. 2-12 for the SN74154 decoder. The SN74155 decoder has also been included (Fig. 2-13) since it has two sections, but the address inputs, A and B, are common to both of the decoder sections. Each section in the SN74155 has separate control or enabling inputs.

A large decoder such as the SN74154 4-line to 16-line decoder provides broad address decoding flexibility. A single SN74154 decoder may be used to nonabsolutely decode 16 addresses, and when either $\overline{\text{IN}}$ or $\overline{\text{OUT}}$ is used as one of the enable inputs, the SN74154 may be used to directly generate 16 device select pulses, without the need for additional gating. This is shown in Fig. 2-14.

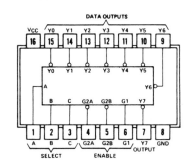

'LS138, 'S138

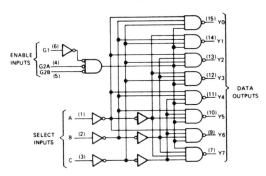

Fig. 2-11. SN74LS138 decoder.

A second decoder may be added to the circuit so that absolute device select pulses are directly generated. A typical example of this is shown in Fig. 2-15. Either $\overline{\text{IN}}$ or $\overline{\text{OUT}}$ may be used to gate or enable the lower decoder. The NOR gates have been used to gate together the *address selection* from the upper decoder and the *address selection plus the function pulse* from the lower decoder. Thus the upper decoder for address bits A7-A4 "qualifies" the address to make the outputs of the NOR gates absolute for addresses 0 through 4. This circuit will work well, but it is not particularly useful.

functional block diagram and schematics of inputs and outputs

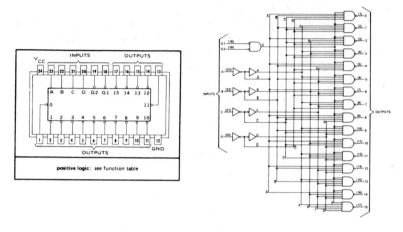

FUNCTION TABLE

INPUTS						OUTPUTS															
G1	G2	D	C	B	A	0	1	2	3	4	5	6	7	8	9	10	11	12	13	14	15
L	L	L	L	L	L	L	H	H	H	H	H	H	H	H	H	H	H	H	H	H	H
L	L	L	L	L	H	H	L	H	H	H	H	H	H	H	H	H	H	H	H	H	H
L	L	L	L	H	L	H	H	L	H	H	H	H	H	H	H	H	H	H	H	H	H
L	L	L	L	H	H	H	H	H	L	H	H	H	H	H	H	H	H	H	H	H	H
L	L	L	H	L	L	H	H	H	H	L	H	H	H	H	H	H	H	H	H	H	H
L	L	L	H	L	H	H	H	H	H	H	L	H	H	H	H	H	H	H	H	H	H
L	L	L	H	H	L	H	H	H	H	H	H	L	H	H	H	H	H	H	H	H	H
L	L	L	H	H	H	H	H	H	H	H	H	H	L	H	H	H	H	H	H	H	H
L	L	H	L	L	L	H	H	H	H	H	H	H	H	L	H	H	H	H	H	H	H
L	L	H	L	L	H	H	H	H	H	H	H	H	H	H	L	H	H	H	H	H	H
L	L	H	L	H	L	H	H	H	H	H	H	H	H	H	H	L	H	H	H	H	H
L	L	H	L	H	H	H	H	H	H	H	H	H	H	H	H	H	L	H	H	H	H
L	L	H	H	L	L	H	H	H	H	H	H	H	H	H	H	H	H	L	H	H	H
L	L	H	H	L	H	H	H	H	H	H	H	H	H	H	H	H	H	H	L	H	H
L	L	H	H	H	L	H	H	H	H	H	H	H	H	H	H	H	H	H	H	L	H
L	L	H	H	H	H	H	H	H	H	H	H	H	H	H	H	H	H	H	H	H	L
L	H	X	X	X	X	H	H	H	H	H	H	H	H	H	H	H	H	H	H	H	H
H	L	X	X	X	X	H	H	H	H	H	H	H	H	H	H	H	H	H	H	H	H
H	H	X	X	X	X	H	H	H	H	H	H	H	H	H	H	H	H	H	H	H	H

H = high level, L = low level, X = irrelevant

Fig. 2-12. SN74154 decoder.

Since each decoder has two enabling inputs, G1 and G2, the NOR gates shown in Fig. 2-15 may be eliminated by using the second enable input on the lower decoder. This enable input is connected as shown in Fig. 2-16. In this circuit, the lower decoder is only enabled when the upper decoder decodes 0000 on address bits A7-A4 *and* when the function pulse $\overline{\text{IN}}$ is present. A second decoder could also be used for $\overline{\text{OUT}}$ device select signals. Note the use of inverters to provide positive (logic one) device select pulses in this case.

Many decoder schemes are possible, and you will have an opportunity to explore the use of several in the experiments. The main

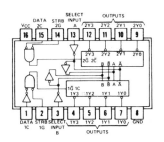 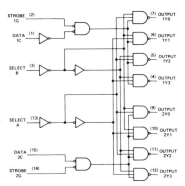

FUNCTION TABLES 2-LINE-TO-4-LINE-DECODER OR 1-LINE-TO-4-LINE DEMULTIPLEXER

INPUTS			OUTPUTS			
SELECT		STROBE	DATA	1Y0	1Y1	1Y2	1Y3
B	A	1G	1C				
X	X	H	X	H	H	H	H
L	L	L	H	L	H	H	H
L	H	L	H	H	L	H	H
H	L	L	H	H	H	L	H
H	H	L	H	H	H	H	L
X	X	X	L	H	H	H	H

(Second function table, right-hand side)

INPUTS			OUTPUTS			
SELECT		STROBE	DATA	2Y0	2Y1	2Y2	2Y3
B	A	2G	2C				
X	X	H	X	H	H	H	H
L	L	L	L	L	H	H	H
L	H	L	L	H	L	H	H
H	L	L	L	H	H	L	H
H	H	L	L	H	H	H	L
X	X	X	H	H	H	H	H

Fig. 2-13. SN74155 decoder.

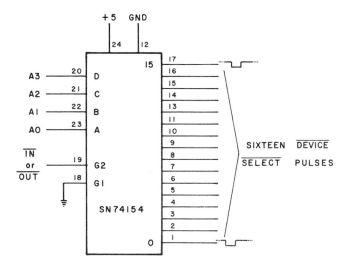

Fig. 2-14. SN74154 decoder used to produce 16 nonabsolute decoded device select pulses.

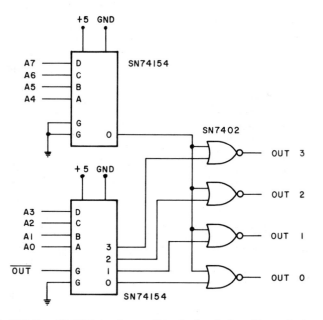

Fig. 2-15. Two SN74154 decoders used for absolute device address selection.

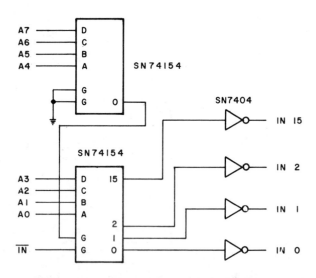

Fig. 2-16. Two SN74154 decoders used to eliminate additional device address gating.

point is that decoders simplify the process of device selection and gating. Decoders are generally used in situations that require flexibility and the generation of several device address signals in proximity to one another.

Using Comparators

The use of digital comparators for device address detection will be the last technique discussed. The comparator-based schemes are relatively straightforward and they are very similar to the "programmable-gate" scheme shown in Fig. 2-3. Remember that comparators, too, are simply collections of gates, connected or integrated, to perform a comparison function. The comparator circuits allow us to preset an address that is constantly compared to the 8-bit values on the address bus. The comparison is done by gating circuits in the comparator chips. A typical comparator is the SN7485 four-bit magnitude comparator, shown in Fig. 2-17. Besides the equal condition, the SN7485 can also detect the greater-than and less-than conditions, but these are not used in address comparison. CAUTION: The *SN74L85 version of the SN7485 chip is not a pin-for-pin equivalent.* Consult a manufacturer's data sheet for additional information.

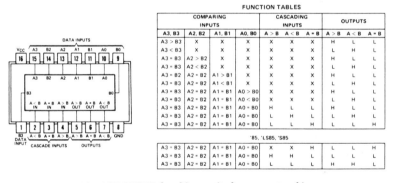

FUNCTION TABLES

COMPARING INPUTS				CASCADING INPUTS			OUTPUTS		
A3, B3	A2, B2	A1, B1	A0, B0	A > B	A < B	A = B	A > B	A < B	A = B
A3 > B3	X	X	X	X	X	X	H	L	L
A3 < B3	X	X	X	X	X	X	L	H	L
A3 = B3	A2 > B2	X	X	X	X	X	H	L	L
A3 = B3	A2 < B2	X	X	X	X	X	L	H	L
A3 = B3	A2 = B2	A1 > B1	X	X	X	X	H	L	L
A3 = B3	A2 = B2	A1 < B1	X	X	X	X	L	H	L
A3 = B3	A2 = B2	A1 = B1	A0 > B0	X	X	X	H	L	L
A3 = B3	A2 = B2	A1 = B1	A0 < B0	X	X	X	L	H	L
A3 = B3	A2 = B2	A1 = B1	A0 > B0	H	L	L	H	L	L
A3 = B3	A2 = B2	A1 = B1	A0 < B0	X	H	L	L	H	L
A3 = B3	A2 = B2	A1 = B1	A0 = B0	L	L	H	L	L	H

'85, 'LS85, 'S85

A3 = B3	A2 = B2	A1 = B1	A0 = B0	X	X	H	L	L	H
A3 = B3	A2 = B2	A1 = B1	A0 = B0	H	H	L	L	L	L
A3 = B3	A2 = B2	A1 = B1	A0 = B0	L	L	L	H	H	L

Fig. 2-17. SN7585 four-bit magnitude comparator chip.

A typical address-comparison scheme is shown in Fig. 2-18, in which the comparator has been preset for address 205 or 11001101_2. Like an 8-input gate circuit, this scheme can detect only a single address, so most comparators are used with decoders for a flexible decoding scheme, as shown in Fig. 2-19. The unique "equal condition" output of the SN7485 is a logic one, so it has been inverted to be compatible with the logic zero requirement of the SN74154 decoder enable input. In this example, the outputs from the SN-

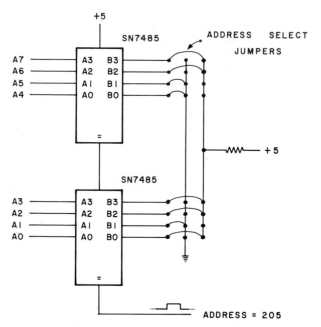

Fig. 2-18. Two SN7485 comparators used to detect address 205.

74154 decoder are only active when the comparator has detected a match between bits A7-A4 (0010) *and* when the $\overline{\text{OUT}}$ pulse is a logic zero. The decoder again directly generates the absolutely decoded device select pulses. In this case, the decoder generates device select pulses only for output devices with addresss of 32 through 47. Another decoder could be added to this circuit so that input devices could also be selected. If the same comparator circuit was used to enable a second decoder, the input device select pulses would also be for devices with addresses 32 through 47. In some cases, separate circuits for input and output device select pulse generation may be used.

This completes our discussion of device addressing, function pulses and device selection. In future examples, we will expect that you will recognize the notation $\overline{\text{OUT}}$ 123 as a logic zero device select pulse, generated through the proper combination of $\overline{\text{OUT}}$ and address 123. The actual gating may be shown, but in most cases, it will be assumed.

You will probably see other device selection circuits in other books, schematic diagrams, etc., but they will all function in the same way, gating an address with a function pulse to select or control a specific device.

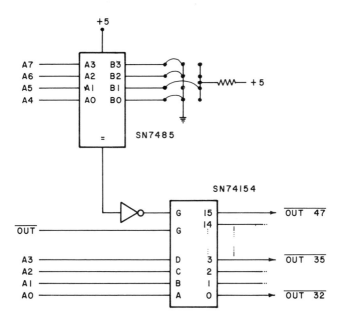

Fig. 2-19. Comparator and decoder used for device selection.

In some experiments, you will explore the use of the device select pulses to control devices. In the next chapter, you will learn
how these pulses are used to control the flow of 8-bit data bytes
on the data bus of the Z-80.

3

I/O Device Interfacing

Now that we have developed a number of ways of selecting and identifying I/O devices, the actual construction and configuration of the I/O ports becomes very important. In this section, we will develop some of the actual bus interfacing schemes that will allow I/O devices to transfer 8-bit bytes to the computer and to receive bytes transferred to them from the computer. As we found with the device selecting circuits, there are many circuits for input ports and output ports. Only a few sample circuits will be provided to illustrate the basic interfacing principles.

OUTPUT PORTS

Output ports are the devices that receive data bytes from the computer, controlled by OUT commands in BASIC-language programs. You have already seen that there is a definite timing relationship between data on the data bus, the $\overline{\text{OUT}}$ pulse and the device address, when an OUT command is executed. This has been shown in Fig. 1-3. In the TRS-80 computer, the duration of the $\overline{\text{OUT}}$ pulse is 1300 nanoseconds. If we use the $\overline{\text{OUT}}$ pulse to gate the data from the data bus to an output device, through the use of the device select pulse, the data is only presented to the output port for 1300 nanoseconds. This period is hardly long enough to allow the data receiving device to perform a meaningful function. To eliminate this problem, each output port must be equipped with some sort of circuit that can acquire data from the bus and "hold" it for as long as needed, or until it is "updated" by another output data transfer.

The type of circuit that can perform this function is called a *latch*, since it can latch the information and hold it until it is updated, or until the power is turned off. There are many different types of latch integrated circuits that offer different configurations of control and data inputs and outputs. Rather than describe all of the various types of latches, we have chosen to describe three general-purpose devices, the SN7475, the SN74175, and the SN-74LS373. The pin configurations and function tables are shown in Fig. 3-1. While the SN7475 and SN74LS373 are true latch devices, the SN74175 really contains flip-flops. The SN7475 latch chip contains four latch circuits and the SN74175 contains four flip-flop circuits, so two SN7475 or two SN74175 chips are required for each 8-bit output port. The 74LS373 contains eight latch circuits, so only one of these is required to construct an 8-bit output port.

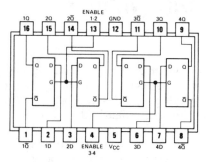

FUNCTION TABLE
(Each Latch)

INPUTS		OUTPUTS	
D	G	Q	$\bar{Q}$
L	H	L	H
H	H	H	L
X	L	Q_0	$\bar{Q}_0$

H = high level, L = low level, X = irrelevant
Q_0 = the level of Q before the high-to-low transition of G

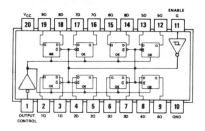

'LS373, 'S373
FUNCTION TABLE

OUTPUT CONTROL	ENABLE G	D	OUTPUT
L	H	H	H
L	H	L	L
L	L	X	Q_0
H	X	X	Z

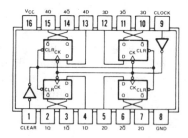

FUNCTION TABLE
(EACH FLIP-FLOP)

INPUTS			OUTPUTS	
CLEAR	CLOCK	D	Q	$\bar{Q}$ †
L	X	X	L	H
H	↑	H	H	L
H	↑	L	L	H
H	L	X	Q_0	$\bar{Q}_0$

Fig. 3-1. Pin configurations and function tables for SN7475 (top), SN74LS373 (middle), and SN74175 (bottom) latch chips.

Let us briefly describe the operation of these latch circuits, so that their use becomes apparent. We will use the SN7475 latch chip as an example. The SN7475 latch circuits can be thought of as "gates that remember." This is shown in the function table for the SN7475 latch, shown in Fig. 3-1. In examining this function table, you will note that when the enable input (G) is a logic one, the data, or logic level present at the "D" input, is passed through the latch to the "Q" output. The Q̄ output is the inversion of the Q output. When the enable input goes from a logic one to a logic zero, the level present at the D input at this time is "latched" or remembered by the Q and Q̄ outputs. The timing relationship shown in Fig. 3-2 illustrates these relationships.

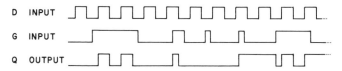

Fig. 3-2. SN7475 latch circuit timing relationships.

As soon as the "G" input goes to the logic one level, the Q output assumes the state of the "D" input even as the levels at the D input change. The logic levels are passed from the D input to the Q output when G is a logic one, and the Q output remains at the level of the D input when G goes to a logic zero. The SN7475 is divided into two sections, each of which can operate independently of the other. These two gate inputs may be connected to make the four latch circuits operate in tandem.

The SN74LS373 operates in the same way as the SN7475, although only one gating or enabling signal is used. In this chip, only the Q outputs are provided. The Q̄ outputs are not provided. An additional output control has been provided, but when used as an output port, this is generally enabled, by grounding (logic zero) the Output Control pin, pin 1.

The SN74175 chip contains four flip-flops that acquire and hold data that are present on the *positive-going* edge of the clock pulse. The logic levels are only updated at this time. Levels are not "gated" through the flip-flops on either the logic zero or logic one level of the clock pulse. A common clear input is also provided, so that the flip-flops may be "cleared" ($Q = 0$, $\bar{Q} = 1$), when this input is taken to the logic zero state. In most cases, the clear input will be connected to +5 volts (logic one) and will not be used.

Each of these integrated circuits may be used to latch and maintain the data put out by the TRS-80 computer during the execution of an OUT command. It is a simple matter of using an output de-

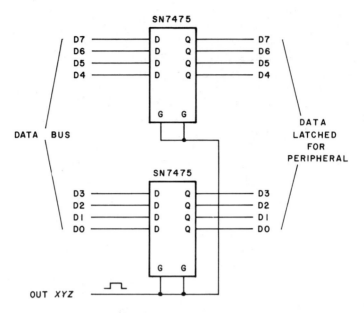

Fig. 3-3. Two SN7475 latch chips used to form an output port.

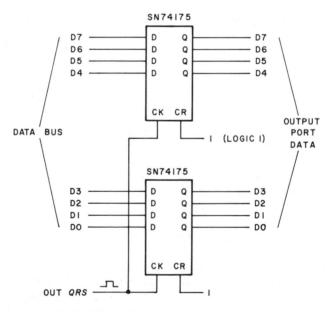

Fig. 3-4. Two SN74175 latch chips used to form an output port.

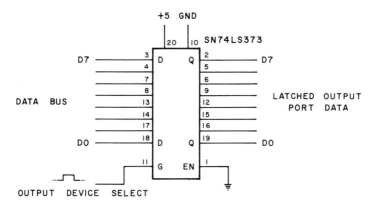

Fig. 3-5. SN74LS373 latch chip used to form an output port.

vice select pulse to activate the latch circuit once it has been connected to the data bus. A typical 8-bit output port is shown in Fig. 3-3. In this circuit, a positive output device select pulse is required to cause the latch circuits to acquire and hold the data output by the TRS-80.

In Fig. 3-4, two SN74175 latch chips have been used as an output port, with standard lamp monitors used to allow a visual indication of the data that have been latched. The "1" indication at the connections to the CLEAR inputs at the output port indicates that these inputs are connected to +5 volts, or a logic one level.

An SN74LS373 8-bit or *octal* latch has been used as an output port, as shown in Fig. 3-5. Only one integrated circuit is required for this output port. The Output Control has been grounded to permanently enable the outputs. Again, an output device select pulse must be supplied from the device selection logic.

Once an output port has been constructed and once it is properly connected to a device select pulse source, it can be accessed under the control of software commands. For example, the command OUT 110,0 would transfer the value zero to output port 110. If an output port is properly selected with an OUT 110 pulse, using one of the types of device selection logic discussed previously, then the value, zero, would be transferred to it.

The program shown in Example 3-1 may be used to generate an increasing binary count at output port 5. The count will continue to sequence (in binary), 254, 255, 0, 1, 2 .... 254, 255, 0, 1, etc. This program will be seen again, in the experiments.

Example 3-1. An 8-Bit Binary Counting Program for Port 5

```
10  FOR N = 0 TO 255
20  OUT 5,N
```

```
30   NEXT N
40   GOTO 10
```

Output ports are rather easy to construct. Most parallel-in, parallel-out logic devices with internal latch capabilities can be used as latches. Examples of devices that can be used at latches are the SN74193 programmable binary counter, the SN74LS194A universal shift register, the SN74198 8-bit shift register, etc.

Most output ports are readily configured with standard integrated circuits. Some newer integrated-circuit devices that are to be used with microcomputers have the output ports or latches already built in.

Typical applications for output ports include the following:

Transfer data to a printer
Transfer data to a video display
Control a traffic light
Transfer data to a floppy disk
Actuate switches on a model railroad
Actuate valves and pumps in a chemical process
Control a plotter
Transfer data to a seven-segment display

In some applications, the *value* of the information is actually used, while in others, the on or off state of each bit is used. Some devices such as a printer may use a combination; ports for the transfer of data and ports for the transfer of on-off control signals. Displays of many digits of information in seven-segment format may require the use of many output ports, even though only one "device" is being controlled.

INPUT PORTS

Input ports are used with I/O devices so that they may transfer information to the computer in 8-bit bytes. Unlike output ports that must be able to accept and hold data at a specific time, and may be continuously connected to the data bus, input ports must be able to "disconnect" themselves from the bus, when they are not in use. The input ports must pass logical information, logic ones and zeros, and they must also be configured so that they do not interfere with the use of the bus, when they are not selected.

Simple gates cannot be used to gate data onto the data-bus lines, since, depending on the type of gate chosen, their "unselect" output state will be a logic one or a logic zero. This is shown in Fig. 3-6. Note that even when none of the gates is selected or enabled, the outputs of the gates generate different logic levels, as noted by the

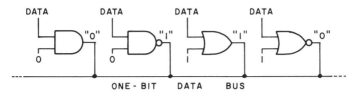

Fig. 3-6. Attempted use of standard gates on a data bus.

quoted logic levels. These levels compete for the use of the bus, probably leading to one or more burned-out chips. This should clearly illustrate why gates alone are not used on data buses.

Special integrated circuits with *three-state outputs* are available to simplify the design of input ports. A typical three-state device is the SN74125 bus buffer, shown in Fig. 3-7. The diagram of the four devices should look familiar. It is simply a buffer (logic one in, logic one out, etc.), but with an additional control line, shown connected to one of the angular sides of the buffer symbol. The buffer will pass logic ones and logic zeros from its input to its output when it is enabled, but unlike a simple gate, when it is disabled, the output appears to be electrically disconnected from the bus, or other logic device, to which it is connected. In three-state devices, this third state is often called the HI-Z or high-impedance state, to note its disconnected state. The disconnecting/connecting is rapid, generally taking less than 20 nanoseconds.

Fig. 3-7. SN74125 bus buffer chip pin configuration.

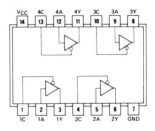

In the SN74125 circuit, each three-state buffer has its own enable input, which must be a logic zero for the data to be passed from the input to the output. A logic one state on the enable input forces the output into the high-impedance state. A similmar integrated circuit, the SN74126, is a pin-for-pin replacement for the SN74125, except that it is enabled with a logic one and disabled with a logic zero. These chips are not often found in microcomputer systems, since more useful devices are available.

For purposes of illustration, a typical bus is shown in Fig. 3-8. In this circuit four one-bit devices have been attached to the bus. Only a one-bit bus is shown for clarity, although in an 8-bit bus

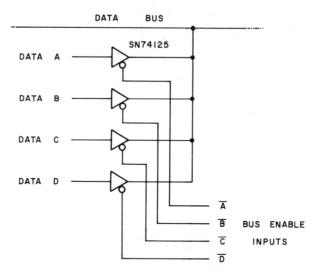

Fig. 3-8. Typical three-state bus for four devices.

system, eight bus lines would be required. When one of the EN-ABLE lines is placed in the logic zero state, the corresponding data bit is passed through the buffer and onto the bus. We will assume that no other devices are connected to the bus. Thus, the truth table shown in Table 3-1 applies.

Table 3-1. Truth Table for a Four-Device Three-State Bus

Enable				Bus Content
D	C	B	A	
1	1	1	1	Undetermined (all devices HI-Z)
1	1	1	0	Data A
1	1	0	1	Data B
1	0	1	1	Data C
0	1	1	1	Data D
0	0	0	0	Not Allowed

When none of the buffers has been enabled or connected to the bus, the bus is not connected to anything except the inputs of the gates, memories, etc., that are the "receivers" of the data bit, so the logic value of the bus is unknown. Whenever a logic zero is applied to one of the buffer enable inputs, *the selected* buffer passes its data onto the bus. The condition in which more than one buffer has been enabled is not allowed, since bus conflicts will arise.

All of the devices that are to be used with the computer system to transfer information to the CPU *must* have three-state outputs.

Thus, even the *memory devices* must have three-state outputs, as they in fact do. The computer designer must be sure that the system has been designed so that no two input devices are selected at the same time. If such a multiple selection takes place, improper operation of the computer occurs.

Input ports that may be used to transfer data to the computer are readily constructed using standard three-state integrated circuits. In most cases, eight individual three-state buffers are used, one per data-bus line. In most cases, too, the enable inputs are all connected in parallel so that all eight bits are transferred to the data bus at the same time. In some cases, this common enable connection is provided within the three-state integrated circuits so that only a single enable pin is used to control all eight bits.

There are many "chips" that may be used to construct input ports, but only a few of them are general enough to warrant our consideration. The two main three-state integrated circuits that will be used in our examples are the SN74365 and the SN74LS244. The SN74365 may also be noted as the DM8095 (National Semiconductor Corp.), which is an exact replacement. The pin configuration for these two circuits is shown in Fig. 3-9.

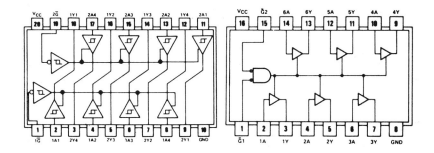

Fig. 3-9. SN74365 (DM8095) and SN74LS244 three-state bus driver chip pin configurations.

You will note quickly that, while the SN74LS244 has eight three-state buffers on one chip, the SN74365 has only six. If the SN74365 device is to be used to construct an input port, two of the integrated-circuit packages must be used. A typical 8-bit input port is shown in Fig. 3-10. In this case, only two of the three-state buffers in the lower SN74365 chip have been used. Since the SN74365 chips contain built-in NOR gates that control the enabling of the three-state buffers, these have been used to combine the $\overline{\text{IN}}$ function pulse and the device address, $\overline{010}$. If the device select signal,

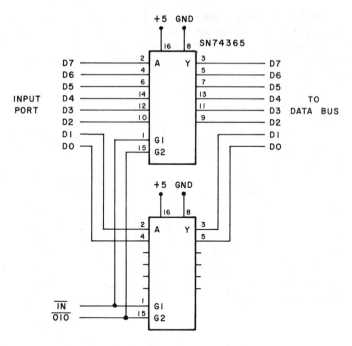

Fig. 3-10. Typical input port constructed using SN74365 chips.

IN 010, had already been generated elsewhere, it could be applied to one of the enable control inputs on both chips, while the others were grounded. The alternate control scheme is shown in Fig. 3-11.

Using such an input port, data values may be input to the com-

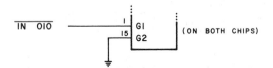

Fig. 3-11. Alternate control scheme for SN74365 three-state chips.

puter through the use of the INP command, as shown in Example 3-2.

Example 3-2. Data Input Program for Port 10

```
10  A = INP (10)
20  PRINT A
30  GOTO 10
```

In this example, the 8-bit binary value is converted into a decimal number between zero and 255 when it is input by the TRS-80 using the INP command at line 10 in the program. It is then printed. It would have been just as valid to use the following command:

10 PRINT INP (10): GOTO 10.

A similar input port may be constructed by using an SN74LS244 octal (8-bit) buffer. This chip contains two independent sets of four buffers each, which are independently controlled with two enable inputs $\overline{2G}$ and $\overline{1G}$. Since no built-in NOR gate is present on the SN-74LS244, external device select gating is required. A typical input port in which an SN74LS244 chip has been used is shown in Fig. 3-12. Software steps similar to those shown in Example 3-2 would be used to control the flow of information from this port into the computer.

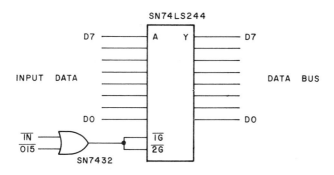

Fig. 3-12. Input port configured with an SN74LS244 chip.

Both the SN74365 and the SN74LS244 have pin-for-pin equivalents that *invert the data bits* as they are passed through the chips and onto the data bus. These inverting buffers are the SN74366 (DM8096) and the SN74LS240, respectively. In most cases, the non-inverting buffers will be the ones used.

In some cases, peripheral devices may generate more than eight bits of information that must be read by the computer. When more than eight bits are to be input, the information is divided into groups of eight bits each. The information is then transferred to the computer one byte at a time. A 16-bit value would require the use of two input ports, as would a 9-bit value. When not all eight bits in an input port are used, the unused bits are often placed in the logic zero state, or grounded. When not all of the bits have actually been implemented, as shown in Fig. 3-13, the unused bits may also be set to a logic zero through the use of appropriate software commands. This will be demonstrated in one of the experiments.

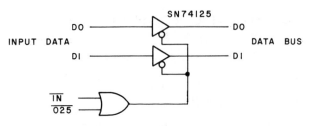

Fig. 3-13. Two-bit input port.

Since a 16-bit number may represent values between 0 and 65,535, some means must be found for converting the individual bytes that are input separately into a single value. Thus, the two values that are each between 0 and 255 must be converted to one value between 0 and 65,535.

Software steps are generally used to implement bits. A simple program that will make the necessary conversion for a 16-bit number is shown in Example 3-3.

Example 3-3. Program for a Two-Byte to One Value Conversion

```
10   A = INP (7)
20   B = INP (8)
30   C = (B*256) + A
40   PRINT C
50   GOTO 10
```

In this example, input port 7 is used to input the eight least significant bits, while input port 8 is used to input the most significant eight bits. The final value of C is between 0 and 65,535. This program would work for as few as nine bits, if the unused, most significant bits are placed in the logic zero state.

Input ports are used to transfer information to the computer. This information may represent actual decimal values for weight, temperature, resistance, etc., or the information may be interpreted as individual binary bits, representing on/off conditions, full/empty states, etc. Typical uses for input ports would be for the:

Transfer of traffic light control information to the computer

Transfer of data from a digital instrument to the computer

Transfer of status (on-off) bits from a printer to the computer

Thet main requirement for input ports is that their outputs have three states.

MEMORY-MAPPED I/O

When standard device addressing was used to address input and output ports, 8-bit addresses were "selected" or decoded and combined with either the $\overline{IN}$ or the $\overline{OUT}$ function pulse to select the

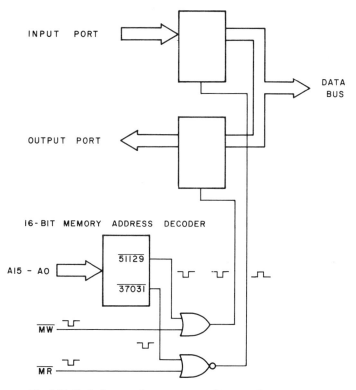

Fig. 3-14. Block diagram of memory-mapped input and output port.

proper port. The INP and OUT commands were used to access the I/O ports under software control.

There is no reason why an output port, or an input port cannot be controlled by a combination of the memory control signals $\overline{MR}$ or $\overline{MW}$ and a decoded 16-bit address. Very simply, this would mean that the PEEK and POKE instructions would be used, instead of the INP and OUT commands. The same commands that are used to access the memory are now used to control I/O ports, too. The mean difference between device addressing and memory addressing is the use of different function pulses, and the decoding of the entire 16-bit address. Since this is the same process that is used in memory chips, it is called *memory-mapped I/O*.

In the TRS-80 computer, there is little to recommend the use of memory-mapped I/O instead of device addressed I/O. In fact, the latter is probably the simpler. In some computers, such as those based on the 6502 or 6800 processor chips, memory-mapped I/O is the only type of I/O control available. When programming in assembly language, there may be situations where memory-mapped I/O has advantages over device addressed I/O.

The block diagrams for an input port and an output port that are controlled as memory-mapped I/O devices is shown in Fig. 3-14. In any case, output ports are constructed from latches and input ports are constructed from three-state buffers.

4

Flags and Decisions

In almost all the previous examples, we have assumed that there is little synchronization required between the computer and the external I/O devices. Thus, output ports have been assumed to always be ready for more data to be transferred to them. In the case of input ports, we have assumed that the data values are present, and ready for transfer to the computer, when the computer reaches the appropriate INP command in a program. This may not always be the case. We must often deal with I/O devices that are slower than the computer.

I/O DEVICE SYNCHRONIZATION

Since not all I/O devices may be ready for the computer at all times, a means of synchronizing the computer and the I/O devices is required. This synchronization generally involves the use of signals that are called *flags*. These signals are used to indicate that various devices are busy or not busy, ready or not ready, converting or not converting, and so on. Thus, "flags" indicate the status of devices, and they are often called *status flags*.

For illustrative purposes, we will assume that we are required to interface a device to a TRS-80 computer. The device will provide 8-bit data values to the computer on an irregular basis. In most cases, such devices also generate a flag signal that indicates that the device is ready to transfer its information to the computer. Such a device is shown in Fig. 4-1. Note that a standard three-state input port has been used to transfer the information to the computer. The ready flag presents an interesting problem. How is the computer going to monitor or check the condition of the READY flag, so that it can determine when a new data value is ready?

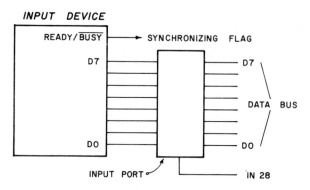

Fig. 4-1. Simple input device with synchronizing flag output.

As we stated previously, there is no rule that limits input ports to the transfer of actual numeric values. The computer has no way of knowing that the 8-bit value, 01100100_2, represents 100, rather than five devices being off, and three devices being on. Thus, another input port could serve quite well as a way of transferring the status flag of the input device to the computer. The other seven bits at this input port may be unused, or they may be used to indicate the status of other external devices. In this way, software steps may be used to check the status of external devices.

When the state of a flag is checked in a computer program, the computer may be programmed to wait until a flag has changed to a particular state before going on with the required action, or it may be programmed to check the flag periodically, going on about other tasks in the meantime.

The logical operations that are available in Level II BASIC are particularly useful in allowing us to check the status of individual flags, or bits, in an 8-bit byte. In this way, the actual logic zero or logic one state of flags may be detected, with the computer making decisions based on the state of the flag.

LOGICAL OPERATIONS AND FLAGS

Probably the most useful logical operation, where flag detection is concerned, is the logic AND operation. You should recall that two bits, A and B, may be "ANDed" together, as shown in Fig. 4-2.

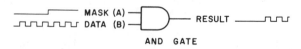

Fig. 4-2. Representation of logical AND operation, using DATA and MASK to yield RESULT.

The result indicates that only when both of the bits are logic ones will the result be a logic one. Another way to think of this is to treat the "A" bit as a "mask," and the "B" bit as information or data. When the mask is a zero, the result is zero. When the mask is a one, the data is passed through to the result. In this way, selected bits may be masked, while other bits are "passed through" the mask.

If, for example, we wished to check the state of bit D5 in the data word, 00111010, a mask of 00100000 could be used. The mask is ANDed with the data word, as shown in Fig. 4-3, for several dif-

VALUE	00111010	00011010	11110000	00011111
MASK	00100000	00010000	00100000	00100000
RESULT	00100000	00010000	00100000	00000000

Fig. 4-3. Example of AND operation in which eight bits of data are operated on.

ferent data words. In all cases, the logic state of D5 was passed through to bit D5 in the result. All of the other bits were masked, or set to zero. In this way, the result was zero, when bit D5 was a logic zero, and the result was one when bit D5 was a logic one. This could be used as the basis for decision making steps in a program. You must remember to convert the masks to their decimal equivalent. In this case, the mask would be equal to 32.

FLAG-DETECTING SOFTWARE

Once an interface has been constructed so that the states of the various flags may be detected, as shown in Fig. 4-4, software may be used to make decisions based on the state of the flags. The pro-

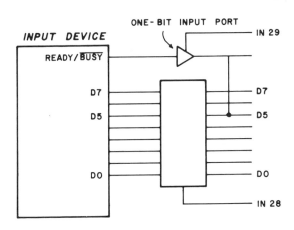

Fig. 4-4. Complete interface in which the flag is detected by software.

gram shown in Example 4-1 shows how a logic zero causes the computer to transfer control to statement 200, while the program shown in Example 4-2 shows how a logic one causes this "jump" to be performed.

Example 4-1. A Logic Zero Flag Used for Control

```
310   A = INP(29)
320   IF (A AND 32) = 0 THEN 200
330   .....Continue here if flag = logic one
```

Example 4-2. A Logic One Flag Used for Control

```
310   A = INP(29)
320   IF (A AND 32) > 0 THEN 200
330   ..... Continue here if flag = logic zero
```

In either case, when the proper flag condition was met, the program would probably input the 8-bit data from port 28 and then wait for the next value to be ready. While this has served as an illustration, flags are often used by themselves, to indicate the state of valves, doors, controls, switches, and other devices, that may not have any data byes associated with them. You will see examples of this in the experiments at the end of this book.

COMPLEX FLAGS

At this point, you may be asking, if the flag on the input device (Fig. 4-4) is used to indicate the availability of an 8-bit value, how does the device know when the computer has input, or accepted, the value that it made available? In some cases, a signal from the computer to the I/O device is used to indicate that the flag had been detected, and that the necessary action had taken place. This signal "clears" the flag. The flag clearing action may be performed by a separate signal, or a signal such as the IN 28 pulse may serve a dual purpose; the enabling of an input port, and the clearing of the flag. This is shown in a simplified timing diagram, Fig. 4-5.

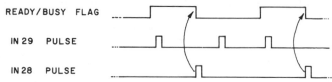

Fig. 4-5. Flag timing diagram.

When the flag is placed in the logic one state, this indicates that the input device is ready to transfer the 8-bit value to the computer. The IN 29 pulse represents the transfer of the *flag status* to the computer. Based on the state of the flag (logic one), the computer executed the steps that transferred the data value through the use

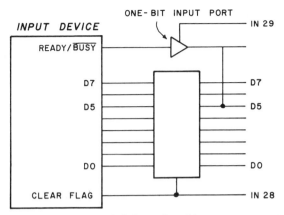

Fig. 4-6. Complete flag circuit in which flag is cleared by computer-generated pulse.

of an INP(28) statement. The pulse generated to enable the three-state input port of the data also cleared the flag.

The second IN 29 pulse again read the status of the flag, but it was a logic zero, so no data was to be transferred. A schematic diagram for the complete interface is shown in Fig. 4-6.

Example 4-3. A Simple Flag Testing Program

```
50  IF (32 AND INP(29)) = 0 THEN 50
60  Q = INP(29)
70  .....Continue the program here
```

Typical devices that use flags in this way are keyboards, floppy disc controllers, analog-to-digital converters, etc.

FLAG CIRCUITS

In some cases, devices may not have the necessary flag circuits within them for easy flag control, or they may not generate logic levels such as those associated with switches, valves, etc., where the logic levels may be present for long periods in one state. In these cases, the "flag" may be a very short pulse. In fact, some flag pulses may be too short to be detected by the computer if the flags are just connected to an input port.

In cases such as this, it is necessary to design a circuit that will "capture" the flag pulse so that it may be detected by the computer sometime later. Even if the computer can test a flag bit every few milliseconds, it will frequently "miss" short pulses of a few microseconds.

Flip-flop or latch circuits are generally used to "remember" the presence of flag pulses. Typical flip-flop devices are the SN7474

D-type flip-flop and the SN7476 J-K flip-flop. We refer you to *Introductory Experiments in Digital Electronics and 8080A Microcomputer Programming and Interfacing*, Book 1, Chapter 11, for a review of flip-flop devices.

A typical flip-flop flag circuit is shown in Fig. 4-7. In this circuit, the input device generates a READY pulse that *clocks* the flip-flop,

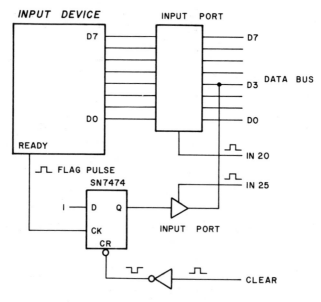

Fig. 4-7. Flip-flop circuit used for detection of flag pulse or level.

transferring the logic level at the D input to the Q output. The Q output is detected by the computer through the use of a second input port, the status of which may be tested, as noted previously. Once the necessary action has taken place, in this case, the input of data from input port 20, the flag flip-flop is cleared. A logic zero pulse, $\overline{\text{CLEAR}}$, serves this purpose. While the inverted IN 20 pulse could be used, we have shown a separate CLEAR pulse, so that the timing may be shown, as in Fig. 4-8.

In this timing diagram, the READY pulse sets the flip-flop, so that its Q output is a logic one. This is detected when the flag status information is input from input port 25. The logic one state of the flag causes the software to perform steps that input the data and then clear the flag. The separate clear pulse could be generated by an OUT command, and appropriate circuitr, although the use of the inverted IN 20 signal is probably easier.

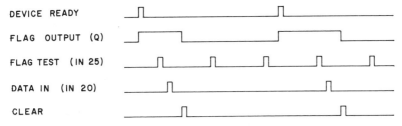

DEVICE READY	
FLAG OUTPUT (Q)	
FLAG TEST (IN 25)	
DATA IN (IN 20)	
CLEAR	

Fig. 4-8. Flag flip-flop timing diagram.

In this example, the flag was tested twice while it was in the logic zero state. Since this indicated that no new data was ready, no input transfers or flag clears were initiated.

Several experiments at the end of this book concern the use of flags.

MULTIPLE FLAGS

Many systems have a number of different flags that must be checked. In some cases, a priority must be established, since some devices are more important, or require faster attention, than do others. The priority is easily set in the program, since the order in which the various bits are tested determines which devices are "serviced" before others. The program steps shown in Example 4-4 will check the flags in sequence, from bit D7 through bit D0.

Example 4-4. Flag Priority Software Steps

```
300   A  =  INP(100)
310   IF (A AND 128) > 0 THEN 1050
320   IF (A AND 64)  = 0 THEN 20
330   IF (A AND 32)  > 0 THEN 260
340   IF (A AND 16)  > 0 THEN 1010
  .          .
  .          .
  .          .
380   IF (A AND 1 )  = 0 THEN 805
390   ..... Continue here if no flags are "set"
```

In this case, some flags were "set" in the logic one state (D7, D5, and D4), while others were set in the logic zero state (D6 and D0). This is often dictated by the interface design, or the action required based on the condition of the flags, that is, whether action is taken when the flag is in the logic zero or logic one state. In some cases, action may be required when a device is not-ready.

INTERRUPTS

In some cases, it is necessary for an I/O device to be serviced as soon as it is ready. It may not be able to wait the many milliseconds that the computer may need to check flags, and make decisions based on them. Almost all computers have a means of being interrupted, but in the TRS-80, this is complicated by the need to use assembly-language programs.

Interrupts have been covered elsewhere for 8080-type processors, and we refer you to *The 8800 Bugbook®: Microcomputer Interfacing and Programming* (Bugbook® is a registered trademark of E & L Instruments, Inc., Derby, Connecticut 06418) and *Introductory Experiments in Digital Electronics and 8080A Microcomputer Programming and Interfacing*, Book 2, Howard W. Sams & Co., Inc., Indianapolis, IN 46206. For assembly-language software for interrupts, we refer you to *8080/8085 Software Design*, Book 2, Howard W. Sams & Co., Inc., Indianapolis, IN 46206.

5

Breadboarding with the TRS-80

It has always been our philosophy that computers should be easy to use, both for program development and for hardware or interface development. Since the necessary computer signals for the TRS-80 are available at the left rear access cover on the keyboard console, it was decided to develop some general interface circuits that could be easily constructed and used. A printed-circuit board was developed, containing all of the necessary circuitry for interfacing purposes. A photograph of this interface is shown in Fig. 5-1. While this circuitry could have been breadboarded and then used for experiments, it was felt that this would only provide additional points at which problems could surface.

BASIC BREADBOARD

The basic breadboard contains a number of useful circuits that allow interface designs to be easily set up and tested. The basic sections are Power Supply, Logic Probe, Device and Memory Decoders, Bus Buffers, and Control Circuitry.

Power Supply

The power-supply section of the breadboard may be operated in one of two ways. An external +5-volt power supply may be used, as long as it can supply 1 amp of current, or an external transformer may be used to supply 12.6 volts (ac) to the on-board power-supply circuits. In either case, the breadboard power supply is separate from the TRS-80 computer power supply, and the TRS-80's power

Fig. 5-1. TRS-80 breadboard system.

supply can not be used to supply the power required. A power-supply schematic is shown in Fig. 5-2.

If the on-board power supply is to be used, the 12.6 VAC transformer is connected to pins 1 and 2 on plug number 1 (P1) and the rectifier diodes, D1-D4, the filter capacitor, C1, and the voltage regulator, VR, are all installed. We suggest that a small heat sink be used with the +5-volt regulator. When the breadboard is used in this manner, +5 volts are available at pin 5, and ground is avail-

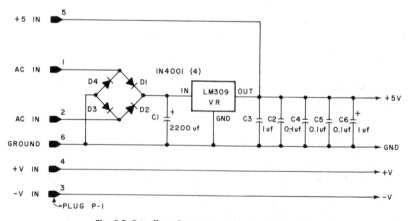

Fig. 5-2. Breadboard power-supply circuit schematic.

able at pin 6, on P1. These connections may be used for external devices, if required.

If a separate +5-volt power supply is to be used, the power-supply parts D1-D4, C1, and VR are not needed, and should be removed, or not installed. The +5-volt and ground connections are made at pin 5 and 6, respectively, at P1.

Since other voltages are often required, such as ±12 or ±15 volts, provisions have been made at P1 to connect additional external power supplies. The positive voltage, +V, and negative voltage, −V, are connected to pins 4 and 3, respectively, at P1.

All of the voltages are available at the socket at position IC-16. The available connections are shown in Table 5-1.

Table 5-1. Power Supply Connections for the Power Socket, IC-16

Pin*	Voltage Available
7,10	+5
5,12	GND
3,14	+V (External)
1,16	−V (External)

* All other pins are unconnected.

Power for the integrated circuits has been derived from the +5-volt power supply. The connections at IC-16 (socket) provide a means of easily obtaining power for the experiments.

Logic Probe

The logic-probe circuit, Fig. 5-3, is useful in determining the logic state of various outputs, and also for detecting pulse activity at outputs. The logic-probe section of the breadboard contains a level detector and a pulse-detector circuit. An LM-319 (IC-15) comparator has been used to detect the logic one and the logic zero levels, while an SN74LS123 (IC-14) has been used to detect and "stretch" pulses. We have used a green LED for the logic zero indicator (D-7), a red LED for the logic one indicator (D-6) and a yellow LED for the pulse indicator (D-5). The input to the probe is available at pins 1-4 at IC socket IC-19. These are marked "P." All of these inputs are in parallel, and any one may be used. (This input should be thought of as two low-power Schottky (LS) input loads.)

If you have an external logic probe, the circuitry in this section may not be required. If you wish, you do not have to construct this portion of the circuit. In any case, it will be useful to be able to detect pulses and also to determine the state of pulses, etc. We have found the logic-probe circuit to be very useful in troubleshooting breadboarded interface circuits.

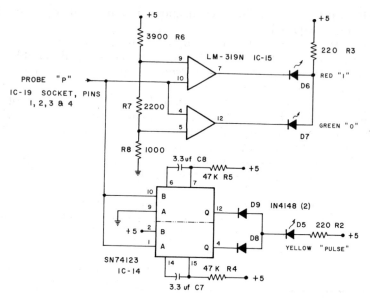

Fig. 5-3. Logic probe circuit schematic.

Device and Memory Decoders

A major portion of the circuitry on the breadboard is devoted to I/O device-address decoding, as shown in Fig. 5-4. The decoders can be operated in either the device mode or the memory mode, depending on whether device addressing, or memory-mapped addressing will be used with I/O devices. In device addressing, the LO address bits (A7-A0) are decoded, while in memory addressing, all of the address bits (A15-A0) are decoded. The schemes used in this portion of the breadboard circuit are a combination of decoder and comparator address-selection circuits.

In the device-addressing mode, an SN74LS85 4-bit comparator, (IC-5), is used to compare preset address bits to the address bits present on the LO address-bus lines, A7-A4. The switch settings are preset using the dual-in-line switch package at IC-6. The positions are clearly marked as "7," "6," "5," and "4" at the switch marked "LO." Be sure that the open or off switch position is to the right (logic one position). Pullup resistors at IC-7 provide for logic one inputs to the SN74LS85 when the switches are open, or in the logic one position.

When an address match occurs between the preset bits and address bits A7-A4, the SN74154 decoder (IC-12) is enabled. Although the SN74154 decoder has the ability to decode address bits A3-A0 into sixteen unique address outputs, only the first eight have

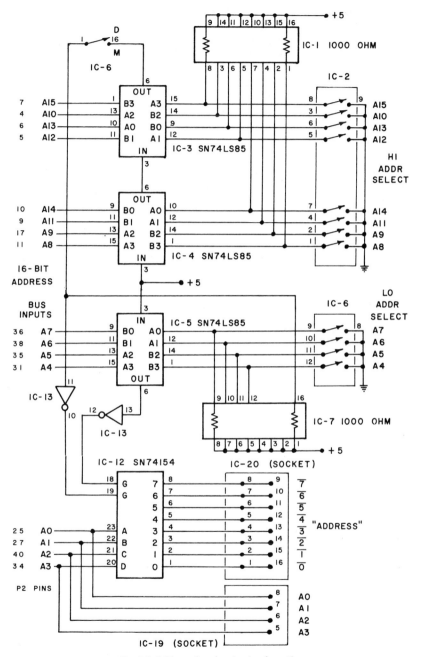

Fig. 5-4. Address decoder circuit schematic.

73

been used, more than enough for breadboarding and interface testing.

Thus, if the address switches for bits 7-4 were set to 1011, the decoder would decode addresses 10110000_2 through 10110111_2 or addresses 176 through 183, decimal. The lowest switch at IC-6, must be "open" or in the "D" position. This places the decoder in the device addressing mode.

The decoded-address outputs are present at the IC-20 socket. They are labeled "0," "1" and so on, through "7." The entire section is called "ADDRESS." Note that there is a bar over the address numbers to indicate that the unique output is a logic zero pulse. The address notation, zero through seven, is a sequential addressing that will help you in determining which pins are connected to which of the selected device addresses. In most cases, these numbers *do not* correspond to actual device addresses. In the addressing example cited previously, in which addresses 176 through 183 were decoded, the output labeled "0" would correspond to the decoded address of 176. Table 5-2 details the decoder outputs that are available at the address socket, IC-20.

Table 5-2. Address-Decoder Connections for the Address Socket, IC-20

Pin (IC-20)	Designation	SN74154 Output Pin
1,16	0	1
2,15	1	2
3,14	2	3
4,13	3	4
5,12	4	5
6,11	5	6
7,10	6	7
8,9	7	8

Connections for address bus lines A3-A0 (unbuffered) are available on the breadboard at pins 8-5, respectively, on the socket at IC-19. These may be used in some experiments, but caution is required, since these are direct connections to the TRS-80 and these four address-bus signals are not buffered on the breadboard.

This address-decoder circuitry will save you much time and effort, since you will not have to construct device address decoders when you wish to implement I/O ports.

Memory addresses may also be decoded on the breadboard. Two additional SN74LS85 comparator chips, IC-3 and IC-4, are used to compare address-bus lines A15-A8 with a preset, 8-bit HI address. The address bits are set at the eight-switch dual-in-line package labeled HI, at IC-2. If memory addressing is to be used, addresses within the range of 0 to 65,535 may be selected, but you should be careful not to select addresses that have been assigned to the internal TRS-80 memory (ROM or R/W).

The complete 16-bit address must be converted to decimal, so that it may be used with the PEEK and POKE instructions. Remember that addresses greater than 32,767 require the use of the formula discussed previously;

$$\text{ADDRESS} = -1^*(\text{DESIRED ADDRESS} - 32767)$$

In the memory address or memory-mapped I/O mode, you must place the lowest switch at IC-6 in the "closed" or in the "M" position. This allows the SN74154 decoder to be activated only when there is a match between address bits A15-A8 and the bits preset at the HI dip-switch *and* a similar match between address bits A7-A4 and the bits preset at the LO dip-switch. Thus, addresses between XXXXXXXX XXXX0000 and XXXXXXXX XXXX0111 are accessible, where X = 1 or 0. These decoded addresses are present as logic zero pulses at the "ADDRESS" socket (IC-20). Remember that only the first eight addresses in a selected 16-address block are available. Thus, if 10000001_2 is set for the HI address and 1110 is set for address bits A7-A4 (LO), addresses 33,248 through 33,256 would generate logic zero pulses at pins 1 through 8 at the "ADDRESS" socket, respectively.

If you are changing between memory (16-bit) addressing and device (8-bit) addressing, you must remember to place the mode switch in the proper position, "M" or "D."

Bus Buffers

Two 8216 noninverting bus buffer chips, IC-1 and IC-11, have been used to buffer the bus, as shown in Fig. 5-5. This means that the bus is available with a full fan-out of 30 (it can power 30 standard SN7400-type inputs) and that it is isolated from the TRS-80 data bus. The eight bits on the data bus are available at the socket at IC-18.

The information in Table 5-3 shows the connection to the data bus.

The bus buffers are always enabled, and the normal mode of operation is for the transfer of data *from the TRS-80 to the breadboard interface*. This means that without additional signal use, you could monitor the bus "activity" by connecting logic probes or logic monitors to all eight data bus outputs, D7-D0. Output ports are implemented by simply using the proper control signals (described in the next section) to control an 8-bit latch. The eight latch inputs are connected to D0-D7 at the socket at IC-18.

Input ports, however, must be implemented so that they turn the bus buffers in the opposite direction to "drive" data into the

Table 5-3. Data Bus Connections at IC-18

Pin (IC-18)	Data Bus Signal
1,16	D7
2,15	D6
3,14	D5
4,13	D4
5,12	D3
6,11	D2
7,10	D1
8,9	D0

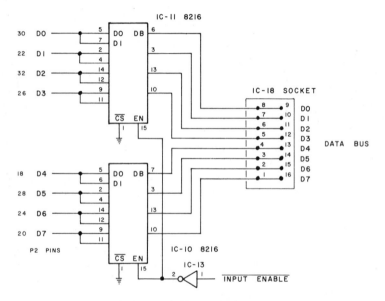

Fig. 5-5. Bus buffer circuit schematic.

TRS-80. Actually there are two bus buffers for each bus line, as shown in the pin configuration shown in Fig. 5-6 for the 8216 buffer. The DIEN input determines which set of buffers is enabled, thus directing data to, or from, the TRS-80. All input operations must activate the proper set of bus buffers so that the TRS-80 receives the data properly. Special control circuitry has been implemented to do this for input operations.

Control Circuitry

The control circuitry on the broadboard is rather simple, consisting mainly of buffers to buffer the six useful control signals output by the TRS-80, $\overline{\text{IN}}$, $\overline{\text{RD}}$, $\overline{\text{OUT}}$, $\overline{\text{WR}}$, $\overline{\text{RESET}}$ and $\overline{\text{INTAK}}$. This is

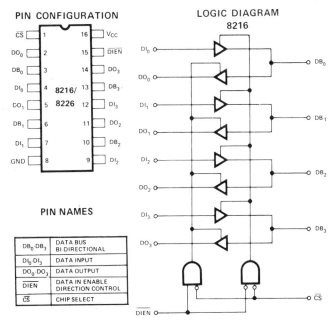

PIN CONFIGURATION

PIN NAMES

DB$_0$-DB$_3$	DATA BUS BI-DIRECTIONAL
DI$_0$-DI$_3$	DATA INPUT
DO$_0$-DO$_3$	DATA OUTPUT
$\overline{\text{DIEN}}$	DATA IN ENABLE DIRECTION CONTROL
$\overline{\text{CS}}$	CHIP SELECT

LOGIC DIAGRAM
8216

Courtesy Intel Corp.

Fig. 5-6. The 8216 Bus Buffer chip pin configuration.

shown in Fig. 5-7. The interrupt input, $\overline{\text{INT}}$, has also been buffered, to protect the computer. Connections to these signals are made at the socket at IC-17, as noted in Table 5-4.

Table 5-4. Control Signal Connections at IC-17

Pin (IC-17)	Control Signal	Direction
1	$\overline{\text{INT}}$	Input
2	Not Used	———
3	INTAK	Output
4	$\overline{\text{RD}}$	Output
5	$\overline{\text{OUT}}$	Output
6	$\overline{\text{WR}}$	Output
7	$\overline{\text{RESET}}$	Output
8	$\overline{\text{IN}}$	Output

You may not be familiar with the $\overline{\text{RESET}}$, $\overline{\text{INTAK}}$, or $\overline{\text{INT}}$ signals. We will only be concerned with $\overline{\text{RESET}}$ at this point, and it is a logic zero pulse, generated when the TRS-80 is turned on or when the reset pushbutton is actuated. All of the control signals are active in the logic zero state, as indicated by the "bar" over their symbol.

The control circuitry also generates a signal that switches the 8216 bus buffers into the input mode, so that data may be transferred into the TRS-80. It would seem to be merely a matter of turning the bus around whenever an input or memory read operation took place. If this were implemented, the bus buffers of the breadboard would be placed in the input mode, even when an input device, or a memory chip was activated within the TRS-80. This would cause a "bus conflict," so the bus on the breadboard must be placed in the input mode only when an input device on the breadboard itself has been selected.

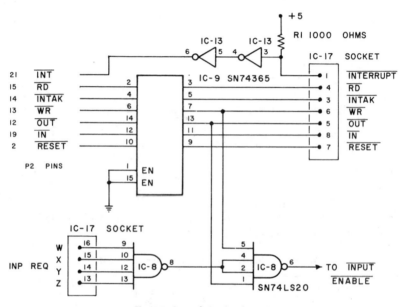

Fig. 5-7. Control circuit schematic.

To handle the input ports properly, the input port device select signal is used to gate data onto the data bus and also to control the mode of the 8216 bus buffers. In effect, up to four input port device select pulses may be "ored" together to place the breadboard bus buffers in the input mode. You will probably not use more than four input ports on the breadboard. Thus, these signals turn the bus buffers around for the input of data only when an input port device select pulse is generated on the breadboard, and it is wired by the user to one of the four bus buffer enable inputs.

The "input request" control pulses are required to be logic zero pulses. They are applied to pins 16, 15, 14, or 13 on the socket at

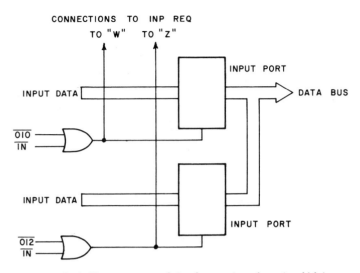

Fig. 5-8. Typical input port control signal generation scheme in which input request signal is generated by each input port.

IC-17. These pins are labeled W, X, Y, and Z in the "INP REQ" section.

Fig. 5-8 shows that these signals for two typical input ports have already been generated to control the three-state input ports, so it is only necessary to connect them also to the W and Z pins in the "INP REQ" signal section of the IC-17 socket (it would have been just as easy to use the X or Y "INP REQ" inputs). Note that two input ports have been illustrated.

The actual ORing of these control signals is performed by the SN74LS20, IC-8. The INPUT REQUEST signal that is output by this four-input NAND gate is further gated with $\overline{OUT}$ and $\overline{WR}$. This gating provides a safety interlock, so that if your breadboard circuits have been improperly wired, the bus buffers cannot be placed in the input mode during output or memory write operations. The resultant "INPUT REQUEST, BUT NOT $\overline{OUT}$ OR $\overline{WR}$" signal controls the input/output mode of the two 8216 buffer chips.

Breadboard Construction

The breadboard circuits may be constructed using wire-wrap techniques, as shown in Fig. 5-9. In this case, the circuits could be expanded and modified through simple wiring changes, but the breadboard itself would be somewhat difficult to use.

To aid in interface construction and testing, a printed circuit has been developed in which all of the necessary circuitry has been

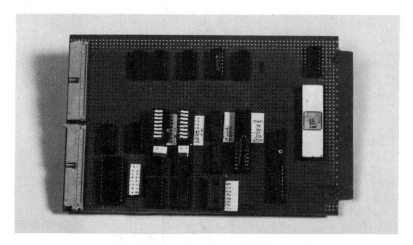

Fig. 5-9. Wire-tapped version of TRS-80 breadboard.

Fig. 5-10. Printed-circuit version of TRS-80 breadboard.

placed on a single board. The power supply and logic probe circuits have been incorporated to make the breadboard easy to use. The breadboard is shown in Fig. 5-10. A large space has been left unused on the breadboard so that a solderless breadboard socket may be mounted directly to the board for easy experimentation. Typical breadboard sockets are the "SK-10" from E & L Instruments, Derby, CT 06418, and the "Super Strip" from AP Products, Inc., Painesville, OH 44077. A complete parts list for the breadboard shown in Fig. 5-10 is provided in the Appendix.

6

TRS-80 Interface
Experiments

The purpose of the experiments in this section is to provide you with some hands-on experience in the use of the latched output port and three-state input port circuits that were developed in the text. You will find that these experiments use simple SN7400-series devices to transfer data to and from the TRS-80 computer.

INTRODUCTION TO THE EXPERIMENTS

Some breadboarding of circuits will be required, and a complete list of the parts that will be used is provided at the end of the experiments If you have not had any hands-on experience in breadboarding digital circuits, we refer you to the first chapter in *Logic and Memory Experiments Using TTL Integrated Circuits* (Howard W. Sams & Co., Inc., Indianapolis, IN 46206). This chapter describes the basic fundamentals of breadboarding. Some auxiliary functions will be required in the experiments to both monitor logic states and to generate them. While we favor the use of the Outboard® modules, similar functions may be readily implemented. In general, we use lamp monitors to indicate logic one (on) and logic zero (off), logic switches to generate logic levels, and debounced pulsers, or pulser for short, that generate logic levels with clean, noise-free transitions between logic levels. Some simple schematic drawings of these types of circuits are provided in the Appendix. In general, most of the experiments in this book can be done with a few simple circuits.

We have provided one experiment that illustrates the use of a decoder circuit for device addressing. While many decoder schemes are possible we feel that one experiment should illustrate the basic principles. If you are interested in other decoder circuits, there are many different ones described in both *The 8080A Bugbook®: Microcomputer Interfacing and Programming* and *Introductory Experiments in Digital Electronics and 8080A Microcomputer Programming and Interfacing, Book 2* (Howard W. Sams & Co., Inc., Indianapolis, IN 46206). In most interface circuits, the decoder scheme that is used on the breadboard will work quite well.

While this book tackles TRS-80 interfacing at a fairly low level, additional writing is planned, covering such topics as interrupts, A/D and D/A converters as well as data processing. The 8-bit input and output ports should serve you quite well, providing a means of transferring information to and from the TRS-80 and the "external world."

The photograph in Fig. 6-1 shows a typical computer-breadboard laboratory station that is used in performing the experiments in this section. A short section of 40-conductor ribbon-cable has been used to connect the TRS-80 and the breadboard. While cable assemblies such as this are available from a number of sources, you must be careful in their use. The cable will have a 40-pin edge connector on one end and a 40-pin "socket header" on the other. These *must* both point in the same direction. Thus, if the cable is placed flat on a table, the openings for the header and edge connector *must* both face in the same direction. This is clearly shown in Fig. 6-2. Other cable arrangements may cause problems in the computer or in the breadboard.

Some experiments will build on, or use, the circuits or programs developed in previous experiments. Please do not turn off your power to the TRS-80, and do not disconnect circuits unless you are instructed to do so. There will be reminders at the end of those experiments in which circuits or programs developed are carried forward.

If you are an instructor planning to use this book as the basis for laboratory experiments, you will find that the programs are readily loaded onto cassettes. In this way, the students spend their time concentrating on the experiment and not on the debugging of the programs. If you choose to use cassettes, you should choose high quality tape, and once the programs have been recorded on the tape, the "write protect" tab on the back edge of the cassette should be removed. This will prevent the students from accidentally recording programs over those already on your tape.

Students may find it valuable to maintain cassettes of their own, so that their lab solutions or other programs are readily available, either for exchange with other students or lab groups, or for reference during the next lab period.

The experiments in this chapter have been divided into two sections, although no division, chapter subheading, or other note marks the sections. The first eleven experiments provide a basic set of interfacing and programming investigations for readers who are interested in basic-interfacing concepts. These first experiments provide a basis for the laboratory portion of a first course in interfacing.

Fig. 6-1. TRS-80 computer and breadboard in experimental use position.

The last seven experiments provide additional lab investigations into more advanced topics, and they also provide projects that may be used to supplement the basic set of experiments. Of course, the entire set of eighteen experiments may be done, too.

EXPERIMENT NO. 1
USE OF THE LOGIC PROBE

Purpose

The purpose of this experiment is to show you how the logic probe circuit on the breadboard may be used to detect logic levels and pulses.

Fig. 6-2. Interfacing cable, note connectors oriented on same side of flat cable.

Discussion

We have assumed that you are using the breadboard logic probe, although other logic-probe circuits will work equally well. The steps in this experiment are useful in helping you to become familiar with the breadboard and the signals available.

Step 1

Your TRS-80 computer should be connected to its video monitor and power supply and it should also be connected to the breadboard through the 40-wire flexible cable jumper. This connection has been described in the introduction to the experiments.

Turn on the power to the computer, video monitor, and breadboard. The computer should print "MEMORY SIZE?" as it normally does. If it does not, turn off the power and obtain assistance in locating the problem.

Step 2

With power applied to the breadboard, connect a jumper wire between one of the pulser input pins, P, at the PROBE socket, to one of the +5-volt pins at the power socket. What is the effect on the logic probe indicators?

The red LED is on, indicating the presence of the logic one state.

The probe jumper wire should now be moved from the +5-volt power pin to a ground, G, pin on the power socket. What is observed, once this connection has been made?

The green LED is on, indicating that the probe input is in the logic zero state. You may have noticed that the pulse detecting LED (yellow) flashed as this connection was made. This flashing state indicates that a logic-level change was detected.

Connect the probe input to address line A0 at IC-19. What do you observe?

All three of the LEDs are on, at different intensities. This is due to the fact that the Z-80 is executing the assembly language instructions in the Level II BASIC ROMs, thus changing the values on the address bus.

Step 3

To test the pulse detecting capability of the logic probe, connect the probe to the $\overline{\text{OUT}}$ pin at the CONTROL SIGNALS socket. What is the logic level there?

The output should be a logic one, since no output operations are being executed by the computer.

Step 4

Enter the following program into your computer and start it. We have assumed that your computer has been initialized and is ready to use:

```
10  OUT 7,255
20  GOTO 10
```

Remember to type RUN and press the ENTER key to start the program. What activity is noted at the logic probe? Why?

The logic probe indicates the presence of continuous pulses, by the P LED being constantly lit. The logic-one LED is also on. This indicates that the normal level is a logic one, but that logic-zero pulses are being detected.

Step 5

Move the logic probe wire to the other six control-signal outputs. Are any others active? Why do you expect the observed behavior?

The $\overline{\text{WR}}$ and $\overline{\text{RD}}$ signals are active. These signals are being generated by the TRS-80 as it executes the short program that you have entered

Do not be surprised by the fact that the WR line is being pulsed. Remember, for the Z-80 to execute the BASIC program, it has to interpret each line or instruction in the program. To do this, the Z-80 has to execute 10s or 100s of assembly language instructions, some of which write information into memory for temporary storage.

Step 6

Change the program to

```
10  A = INP(7)
20  GOTO 10
```

and start it. Do you expect any change in the pulse activity at the $\overline{\text{OUT}}$ pin? Would any of the other I/O control signals be active? Which one?

Since the OUT command is no longer used, the $\overline{\text{OUT}}$ pulse should no longer be observed. You should be able to use the probe to detect pulses at the IN signal pin.

In some of the following experiments, the logic probe will be used to examine outputs and to detect logic states and pulses. This will be noted by, " . . . use your probe to examine . . . ," or perhaps by, ". . . use the logic probe to measure . . . ," etc.

EXPERIMENT NO. 2
USE OF THE DEVICE ADDRESS DECODER

Purpose

This experiment allows you to explore the use of the device address-decoder circuit on the interface printed-circuit board that will be used in some of the future experiments.

Discussion

In this experiment, address A7-A0 will be used by the LO address-decoder section, or device address-decoder section of the breadboard. The logic probe will be used to detect the pulses and states generated by this logic. The solderless breadboard and an SN7402 quad NOR gate integrated circuit are required.

Pin Configuration of the Integrated Circuit (Fig. 6-3)

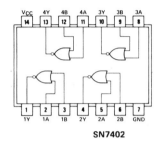

Fig. 6-3. SN7402 NOR-gate chip pin configuration.

SN7402

Step 1

No circuits should be presently wired on your breadboard. If any circuits are present, remove them from the solderless breadboard. In this experiment, the device addressing mode will be used, so be sure that the bottom switch at the LO address DIP switch is in the "D" or off position.

Step 2

Place the DIP switches for address bits A7-A4 in the logic zero position. Can you determine what addresses will cause the SN74154 decoders outputs labeled 0 through 7 to go to a logic zero? You may wish to examine the schematic in Fig. 5-4.

The decimal addresses 0-7 should generate pulses at the respective outputs of the decoder.

Step 3

Start the computer. If it is running a program, press the BREAK key. Use the probe to monitor the eight decoder outputs present at the ADDRESS socket. Are any of the decoder outputs active (pulsing)? Since you are not running a program, is this what you would expect?

Most, if not all, of the decoder outputs are active. While the computer is not running a BASIC program that you have entered, it is executing program steps that monitor the keyboard, etc. Remember that the decoder decodes only address bits A7-A0, and that it is *always* decoding addresses.

Step 4

Wire the circuit shown in Fig. 6-4. Be sure to properly connect the power pin, pin 14, to +5 volts and the ground pin, pin 7, to power-supply ground. The outputs of gates A, B, and C are not connected to any circuit at this time.

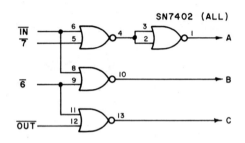

Fig. 6-4. Function pulse-generation circuit.

Step 5

Enter the following program into the computer and run it:

```
10   A = INP(6)
20   GOTO 10
```

Using the logic probe, monitor the $\overline{\text{IN}}$ pulse (pin 6 or 8), the address "6" pin (pin 9 or 11) and the address "7" pin (pin 5). Note your observation below; noting the state of the LEDs of the logic probe.

	Logic 0	Logic 1	Pulse
$\overline{\text{IN}}$			
"6"			
"7"			

Now monitor the logic gate outputs A, B, and C and note any activity, at those points, as determined with the logic probe, in the space below:

	Logic 0	Logic 1	Pulse
A			
B			
C			

Is this what you would expect? Can you explain this?

Yes, this is what is expected, since the input (INP) command in the program specified device "6" as an input device. Thus only output "B" should be active. No output devices were specified in the program.

Step 6

Change the device address in line 10, so that address 15 is selected. Line 10 should now be 10 A = INP(15). Run the program and test gate outputs A, B, and C once again. You should observe that none of these are active. Why?

The address, 15, is not implemented in the circuit. Furthermore, it is not readily accessible on the breadboard. Of the addresses in the block 0 through 15, only addresses 0 through 7 may be obtained at the ADDRESS socket.

Step 7

Change line 10 in the program so that it is now

```
10   A = INP(6) : B = INP(7)
```

Where do you now observe the pulses?

You should find that outputs A and B are active. Output C is not active, since it is an output port control pulse, and there are no OUT commands in the program.

Step 8

Add a statement to the program so that output C is activated, along with outputs A and B. Try it. We added the statement:

and ran the program. All three outputs were activated. Note that outputs B and C are active in the logic one state, while output A is active in the logic zero state. When the probe logic zero LED and pulse LED are both lit, this indicates that the *normal* state is logic zero and a logic one pulse is generated.

Note that even though we only wanted to generate an $\overline{\text{OUT 006}}$ pulse, a data value still had to be specified in the OUT command. Of course, there are no latches in the interface that will "capture" or latch this value.

Step 9

Could you reconfigure the address decoder so that addresses 102 and 103 are generated, rather than addresses 6 and 7? How would you determine this? Are they valid addresses?

Convert these decimal addresses to their binary equivalents, 01100110 and 01100111, respectively. They are both within the first eight addresses, when the address "space" is grouped into blocks of sixteen addresses each (bit A3 = 0), so they are accessible.

How would you set address switches A7-A4 to enable the decoder to decode these addresses? At which ADDRESS outputs would they be found?

Address bits A6 and A5 would have to be preset to logic ones, while bits A7 and A4 remain at logic zeros, so that bits A7-A4 represent 0110. The addresses 102 and 103 would be found at ADDRESS outputs 6 and 7, respectively.

You may test this if you wish, by changing the switch settings, *and* changing your program so that addresses 102 and 103 are used. *Once you have tested this, restore the LO address bits at the DIP switch to 0000.*

Do not remove the circuit from your breadboard at this time. The program will not be used again, so power may be turned off.

EXPERIMENT NO. 3
USING DEVICE-SELECT PULSES

Purpose

In this experiment, you will observe the use of device-select pulses to control an external device. Although generally used to control the flow of information, the INP and OUT commands may also be used to generate useful pulses.

Discussion

In this experiment, a simple device will be turned on and off through the use of device-select pulses. The logic probe will be used as the "device" and a simple bistable flip-flop will be controlled by two software-generated pulses.

Pin Configuration of the Integrated Circuit (Fig. 6-5)

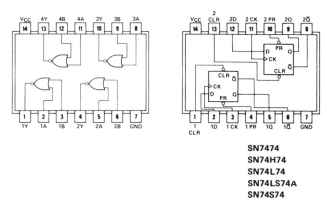

SN7474
SN74H74
SN74L74
SN74LS74A
SN74S74

Fig. 6-5. SN7402 and SN7474 chip pin configurations.

Step 1

The device-select circuit used in Experiment No. 2 is also used in this experiment. If it has not been wired, wire it as shown in Fig. 6-4.

Step 2

Wire the SN7474 flip-flop as shown in Fig 6-6. The "1" noted at the "D" input to the SN7474 indicates a logic one (+5 volts) is applied to this input. Likewise, a "0" would indicate a logic zero, or ground connection. The Q output from the SN7474 should be the only connection to the probe. Remember to make the power connections to the SN7474; pin 14 to +5 volts and pin 7 to ground.

Step 3

In this circuit, the OUT 6 pulse will clock the Q output of the flip-flop to a logic one, while the $\overline{\text{IN 7}}$ pulse will clear it to a logic zero Since a flip-flop is stable in either state, once pulsed by OUT 6, its Q output will remain in the logic one state until power is removed, or until it is cleared to logic zero with an $\overline{\text{IN 7}}$ pulse.

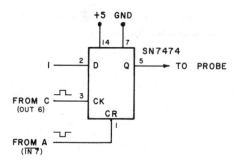

Fig. 6-6. Simple flip-flop controller circuit.

Enter the following program into your computer and run it.

```
10   A = INP(7)
20   OUT 6,0
30   FOR I = 1 TO 300: NEXT I
40   A = INP(7)
50   FOR I = 1 TO 300: NEXT I
60   GOTO 20
```

Disregard the logic probe pulse LED. What is the effect on the logic one and logic zero LEDs?

They flash logic one, logic zero, logic one, etc., in sequence.

Step 4

Alter the time delay routine at line 50 to:

```
50   FOR I = 1 TO 1000: NEXT I
```

When the change has been made, run the program. What is the effect of the change?

The logic zero LED is on for a longer period. Thus, it is possible to generate control pulses that are a known period apart, say 1 second.

Step 5

Can you determine the software delay necessary in a FOR . . . : NEXT statement to generate a 1-second period? Modify your program and test various time delay counts until you closely approximate 1 second. You might want to try for a 10-second period and then divide by 10 for a 1-second period. What delay did you come up with?

We found that a delay statement,

```
FOR I = 1 TO 375: NEXT I
```

required about one second to be executed.

Step 6

You can now use the power of BASIC to allow you to tell the computer how long each LED is to be ON. The following program may be entered and run. It first asks you for the period of each LED, in seconds, and then runs the program.

```
10   A = INP(7)
20   INPUT "RED LED PERIOD ="; Q
30   INPUT "GREEN LED PERIOD ="; R
40   PRINT "TOTAL CYCLE PERIOD IS"; Q + R; "SECONDS"
50   OUT 6,0
60   FOR S = 1 TO Q
70   FOR I = 1 TO 375: NEXT I
80   NEXT S
90   A = INP(7)
100  FOR S = 1 TO R
110  FOR I = 1 TO 375: NEXT I
120  NEXT S
130  GOTO 50
```

When the program is run, the time delays may be somewhat lengthened. Why?

The additional software steps (FOR S = 1 TO Q, FOR S = 1 TO R and NEXT S) add time to the overall execution time of the program. What does this program illustrate?

It illustrates many principles; the use of simple programs and simple circuits to control external devices. It also illustrates the power of BASIC to control external devices through relatively simple software steps. Remember, though, that BASIC is relatively slow.

Even though INP and OUT commands were used, the success of the flip-flop interface *did not depend on the actual transfer of any information.* The flip-flop was controlled, or switched, through the use of the device-select pulses, alone. This principle is often used when a control signal or control pulse is required, but no data is transferred.

The SN7474 flip-flop circuit may be removed. The remaining circuitry should be retained. The program will not be used again

EXPERIMENT NO. 4
CONSTRUCTING AN INPUT PORT

Purpose

The purpose of this experiment is to construct an input port using three-state buffer circuits.

Discussion

The simple 8-bit input port that you will construct as a part of this experiment will provide a means of entering data into the computer. Several additional experiments will use this input port. The device-select circuit used previously will be used in this experiment. The SN74365 or DN8095 three-state buffer will be used.

Pin Configuration of the Integrated Circuit

Step 1

The gating circuitry developed in Experiment No. 2 will be used in this experiment. If this circuit is not present on your solderless breadboard, refer to Fig. 6-4 and wire it. Your computer and breadboard power should be off.

Step 2

Wire the 8-bit input port circuit shown in Fig. 6-8. Two SN74365 (DM8095) three-state integrated circuits are required.

Step 3

Note that in this circuit only one of the two enable inputs on the SN74365 chip is used. The other enable input has been permanently connected to ground (logic zero). Thus, the internal NOR gate of the SN74365 buffer has not been utilized.

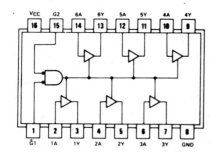

Fig. 6-7. SN74365, or DM8095 three-state buffer chip pin configurations.

Connect the $\overline{\text{DEVICE}}$ $\overline{\text{SELECT}}$ line to point "A" (pin 1 on the SN7402), as shown in Fig. 6-4. This is the signal for IN 7.

The notation LOGIC SWITCHES in Fig. 6-8 is used to represent switches that are used to generate logic one or logic zero states. Simple jumper wires to ground and +5 volts on a solderless breadboard may be used. There is additional information in the Appendix about this type of logical function.

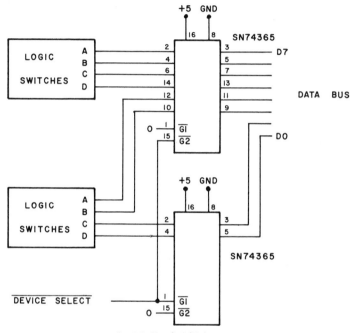

Fig. 6-8. Simple 8-bit input port.

Step 4

Once the input port has been constructed and the device select pulse provided from the SN7402 NOR gate, enter and run the following program:

```
10  PRINT INP(7)
20  GOTO 10
```

What is displayed on the screen? Does changing the logic switch settings have any effect on the data value displayed? Is this what you expect?

The value 255 is displayed, corresponding to 11111111_2. Changing the logic switches had no effect on the data values that were displayed. At first, you might have expected the data values to be input from the interface as wired, but this was not observed. Why?

The interface circuit was not provided with an input request (INP REQ) signal that is used to place the two bus buffers in the input mode.

Step 5

Make a connection between the SN7402 "A" or IN 7, output (pin 1) and the "W" INP REQ pin at the CONTROL SIGNALS socket. This signal will place the 8216 bus buffers in the input mode.

Now that this connection has been made, restart your program and change the switch settings. Are the switch settings reflected in the data? You may wish to test each switch separately.

The switch values are now transferred to the computer and displayed as the decimal equivalents of the binary-switch settings

If you would rather see the values in the binary form, the following program may be run. It will display the binary values continuously.

```
10   A = 128
20   B = INP(7)
30   FOR Q = 1 TO 8
40   IF B-A<0 THEN GOTO 100
50   PRINT "1";
60   B = B-A
65   A = A/2
70   NEXT Q
75   PRINT
80   GOTO 10
100  PRINT"0";
110  GOTO 65
```

If you wish to change a switch setting, and then obtain its binary equivalent, change line 10 to

```
10   INPUT; R : CLS: A = 128
```

Now, whenever you wish to display the binary value of the logic switch setting at the input port, simply depress the ENTER key on the TRS-80 keyboard Of course, the switch settings are already in binary format, so the correlation between the displayed binary value and the switch settings should be easy.

Do not remove the input-port circuitry from your breadboard, and do not destroy the program by turning off the power at this time.

EXPERIMENT NO. 5
MULTIBYTE INPUT PORTS

Purpose

The purpose of this experiment is to show you how multiple bytes may be input and processed using the BASIC program.

Discussion

Not all input devices transfer only one 8-bit byte to the TRS-80. Some I/O devices may require 12 or more bits. In this experiment, you will simulate two input ports through the use of the input port constructed in Experiment No. 4. Refer to Experiment No. 4 for construction details of the input port. We recommend that you work through Experiment No. 4 before proceeding with this experiment, if you have not already performed it.

Step 1

If you do not have an input port connected to your TRS-80 computer, we refer you to Experiment No. 4. The circuit developed in that experiment must be used.

Step 2

In handling multibyte data, the TRS-80 must be programmed so that the various bytes are ordered from most-significant to least-significant byte. In this experiment, we shall use byte "M" as the most-significant byte (MSBY) and "L" as the least-significant byte (LSBY). Since the TRS-80 will input 8-bit values between zero and 255, can you suggest an equation that could be used to obtain the decimal value of a 16-bit word?

Since the MSBY is "offset" by the value of 256, we used the following formula:

$$V = (M*256) + L$$

where V is the final decimal value of the 16-bit data word.

Step 3

To test this equation, enter the following program into the computer:

```
200   INPUT "SET MSBY"; R
210   M = INP(7)
220   INPUT "SET LSBY"; R
230   L = INP(7)
240   V = (M*256) + L
250   PRINT V
260   GOTO 200
```

Now run the program (RUN 200). When the computer asks, "SET MSBY?" set the eight bits for the MSBY of the "16-bit value" on the eight logic switches and depress ENTER. When the computer asks, "SET LSBY?" set the eight bits for the LSBY of the "16-bit value" on the switch register and again depress ENTER. The value of the 16-bit data word, in decimal, should now be displayed on the screen. Some typical 16-bit binary values that you may wish to use are found in the following list. Fill in the decimal values for each, as generated by the TRS-80. You should be able to check these quickly.

MSBY	LSBY	VALUE
11001010	11000001	
11000111	00011101	
00000001	10000001	

You should observe the values 51905, 50973 and 385.

Step 4

The following program is a combination of the binary output program, and the two-byte decimal calculation program. It will allow you to input two 8-bit bytes, display the decimal value, and the binary value.

```
*10   A = 32768
*20   FOR S = 1 TO 2
 30   FOR Q = 1 TO 8
 40   IF B−A<0 THEN GOTO 100
 50   PRINT "1";
 60   B = B−A
 65   A = A/2
 70   NEXT Q
*75   PRINT "      "; :NEXT S
*80   PRINT: GOTO 200
100   PRINT "0";
110   GOTO 65
200   INPUT "SET MSBY"; R
210   M = INP(7)
220   INPUT "SET LSBY"; R
230   L = INP(7)
240   V = (M*256) + L
*250  CLS: PRINT V
*260  B = V: GOTO 10
```

If you already have both programs (Experiment No. 4, Step 5 and Experiment No. 5, Step 3) in the computer, you only need to enter new lines of instructions at the lines noted with an asterisk (*).

Step 5

Run the new program shown in Step 4 (RUN 200), setting different values on the switches for the MSBY and LSBY. The correlation between your switch settings and the binary outputs should be obvious. You should be able to calculate decimal values from the binary settings to check the values computed by the TRS-80.

Now that you are able to transfer 16-bit data to the TRS-80, you should be able to see that the computer could have processed these values in other ways, using them in other calculations. Although only a single-byte input port was used, two input ports could have been used to transfer a 16-bit value to the TRS-80.

The interface will be used in the next experiment, so do not dismantle it. The power may be turned off.

EXPERIMENT NO. 6
INPUT-PORT APPLICATIONS

Purpose

The purpose of this experiment is to show you how the input port may be used for control applications.

Discussion

In this experiment, the 8-bit input port will be used to transfer information to the computer, but the computer will process the eight bits of data in a nonnumeric fashion. In this way, the *state* of eight external devices will be monitored.

Step 1

If you do not have an input port connected to your TRS-80 computer, we refer you to Experiment No. 4. The input port described in that experiment will be used in the following steps.

Step 2

In many cases, the computer will be used to process nonnumeric data that provides information about the status or state of external devices. In such a way, it is easy to determine when devices are on or off, valves open or closed, elevators up or down, etc.

Enter the following program into your computer and run it. This program demonstrates how a value may be used to cause the computer to take a preprogrammed course of action:

```
10   INPUT Z: CLS
20   A = INP(7)
30   IF A>127 THEN GOTO 70
40   PRINT "INPUT < = 127"
50   GOTO 10
70   PRINT "INPUT > 127"
80   GOTO 10
```

Step 3

You must press the ENTER key to cause the computer to execute the input and comparison steps. Set the switches at the input port to a value of less than 127 (00000000 to 01111110) and press ENTER. What happens? Try this with a value of 127 (01111111 to 11111111) or greater. What happens? What happens to the display when the value is equal to 127 (01111111)?

You should observe the correct message, indicating the value of the bits set at the input port. This illustrates how the computer may make a decision based on the overall value, or individual bit in some cases, that we are interested in. The binary conversion program in Experiment No. 4 allowed you to observe the state of the bits, as either logic one or logic zero, decisions being made on the value of each bit position.

Step 4

In this step, the basic binary-display routine will be used, but rather than the display of ones and zeros, the computer will display "ON," for a logic one and "OFF," for a logic zero state. You should be able to modify the program from Experiment No. 4 to do this, just by changing the PRINT statements, but the following listing is provided for you. Note that the program from Experiment No. 4 has been "moved" or relocated to higher line numbers. Before you load this program, remember to delete the old program. The NEW command may be used to do this.

```
110   INPUT Z: CLS: A = 128
120   B = INP(7)
130   FOR Q = 1 TO 8
140   IF B−A<0 THEN GOTO 200
150   PRINT "ON      ";
160   B = B−A
170   A = A/2
180   NEXT Q
190   GOTO 110
200   PRINT "OFF     ";
210   GOTO 170
```

Note: There are four spaces after ON, and three after OFF. This generates equal spacing.

Run the program. Remember that the switches should be set, and then the ENTER key pressed, to perform the "conversion" and display.

You should now observe that the display shows the logic zero state to be OFF, and the logic one state to be ON. The PRINT statement could be changed to generate UP and DOWN, OPEN and CLOSED, or other "binary" messages.

Step 5

While the program in Step 4 has some uses, the display of the ON and OFF messages in column format may be more useful. Make the following changes and additions (*) to your program and run it. Leave the spaces after ON and OFF in lines 150 and 200, respectively.

```
*100  R = 20
 110  INPUT Z: CLS: A = 128
 120  B = INP(7)
 130  FOR Q = 1 TO 8
 140  IF B−A<0 THEN GOTO 200
*150  PRINT@ R, "ON       ";
 160  B = B−A
*170  A = A/2 : R = R +64
 180  NEXT Q
*190  GOTO 100
*200  PRINT@ R, "OFF      ";
 210  GOTO 170
```

You should now observe that the display of OFF and ON states is vertical since the PRINT statements have been replaced by PRINT@ statements.

Thus, the ON and OFF states can be displayed in a number of ways. You may wish to try several settings of switches to confirm that the states are being displayed correctly.

Step 6

The program may be run continuously, simply by removing the INPUT Z: portion of statement 110. Remove this so that the line is now 110 CLS: A = 128 and re-run the program. Does this provide a reasonable display? Why?

Our display flickered, since during each pass through the program, the CLS command cleared the screen, and the PRINT statements had to replace ON and OFF states that were displayed. This was not acceptable.

Step 7

Could you suggest a means of correcting the display flicker? Note the use of the PRINT@ statements, rather than PRINT.

By removing the CLS command, a flicker-free display is generated, the PRINT@ statement leaves the screen alone, but it prints over the words already there; an "ON" printed over an "ON" is still "ON." When ON is printed over OFF, the result will be ONF, unless you left a space in the quoted statement in line 150, "ON." Remember to clear the screen with a CLS command or the CLEAR key before you run the modified program, or the ON and OFF display will be superimposed on whatever is left on the screen.

Step 8

The PRINT@ statements could also be used to generate titles for the eight lines. Several follow, and you may add to or change the ones provided:

```
05   CLS
10   PRINT@ 0,     "ACID PUMP";
20   PRINT@ 64,    "BASE PUMP";
30   PRINT@ 128,   "HEATER";
40   PRINT@ 192,   "MIXER";
50   PRINT@ 256,   "FLUSH CYCLE";
60   PRINT@ 320,   "DISHWASHER";
70   PRINT@ 384,   "VACUUM";
80   PRINT@ 448,   "DRYER";
```

We suggest that you add these lines to your program if you plan to go ahead with Experiment No. 7. You should test your program once these additions have been made.

The hardware and the software used in this experiment will be used in Experiment No. 7. Do not turn off the power to your interface, or to the TRS-80 computer.

EXPERIMENT NO. 7
INPUT-PORT APPLICATIONS (II)

Purpose

The purpose of this experiment is to show you how logical operations may be performed on data.

Discussion

This experiment will use AND operations. These operations will be performed on the ON/OFF information to detect various states or conditions. These conditions may be used to trigger subsequent actions by the computer.

Step 1

The program used in this experiment is the same as the one used in Experiment No. 6. If it has not been completely entered into the computer, you must enter it and test it. If it has been entered and tested in the previous experiment, you may wish to check it against the listing:

```
05   CLS
10   PRINT@ 0,    "ACID PUMP";
20   PRINT@ 64,   "BASE PUMP";
30   PRINT@ 128,  "HEATER";
40   PRINT@ 192,  "MIXER";
50   PRINT@ 256,  "FLUSH CYCLE";
60   PRINT@ 320,  "DISHWASHER";
70   PRINT@ 384,  "VACUUM";
80   PRINT@ 448,  "DRYER";
100  R = 20
110  A = 128
120  B = INP(7)
130  FOR Q = 1 TO 8
140  IF B−A<0 THEN GOTO 200
150  PRINT@ R, "ON      ";
160  B = B−A
170  A = A/2 : R = R + 64
180  NEXT Q
190  GOTO 100
200  PRINT@ R, "OFF     ";
210  GOTO 170
```

When successfully loaded and run, the program should generate a display such as that shown in Table 6-1. The various ON and OFF conditions shown by your computer may be different, depending on the states of the switches in your interface.

Table 6-1. Control Program Output

ACID PUMP	ON
BASE PUMP	OFF
HEATER	ON
MIXER	ON
FLUSH CYCLE	ON
DISHWASHER	ON
VACUUM	OFF
DRYER	OFF

Step 2

Make a series of notes in the following space about which data bits, D7, D6, etc., correspond to the individual device labels. You may do this by examining your interface or through examination of your program.

You should find that the "ACID PUMP" is bit D7 (MSB) and that the "DRYER" is bit D0 (LSB).

Step 3

We now want to modify the program so that it will detect whenever *any* of the appliances, DISHWASHER, DRYER, or VACUUM are on, and whenever the ACID PUMP *and* BASE PUMP are both on. The logical operations will be used, although other solutions might be used, as well.

Can you suggest a method of making these determinations? We suggest that you refer to the "Logical Operators" section of Chapter 8 in your *Level II BASIC Reference Manual* for a review of the AND and OR operations if you are not familiar with them.

The conditions that we wish to detect are shown in Table 6-2.

Table 6-2. Control Conditions to be Detected

D7	D6	D5	D4	D3	D2	D1	D0	
1	1	X	X	X	X	X	X	ACID AND BASE PUMPS BOTH ON
X	X	X	X	X	0	0	1	
X	X	X	X	X	0	1	0	
X	X	X	X	X	0	1	1	
X	X	X	X	X	1	0	0	ANY APPLIANCE ON
X	X	X	X	X	1	0	1	
X	X	X	X	X	1	1	0	
X	X	X	X	X	1	1	1	

X = Don't care, logic one or zero.

Step 4

The logical AND operation can be used to mask out the unwanted bits, D5-D0 for the pump tests and bits D7-D3 for the appliance tests. Thus, two "masks" must be established, one for the pumps, and one for the appliances. What would these masks be, in binary and in decimal?

The mask for the pumps would be 11000000_2, or 192, while the mask for the appliances would be 00000111_2, or 7. When these masks are ANDed with the input value from the switches, the desired bits will be "filtered" through the mask.

Step 5

Now that the masks have been established, suggest some software steps that could be used to determine the state of the "filtered" bits. You should think in terms of both a binary and an equivalent decimal representation of the results of the AND operation.

We have assumed that a variable, C, has also been set to the value from the input port. If you use the variable, B, in program steps after the ON/OFF output section of the program, you will find that it is always zero.

We used either

IF (C AND 7)>0 THEN . . .

or

IF (C AND 7)=0 THEN . . .

to detect the appliances and we used either:

IF (C AND 192)=192 THEN . . .

or

IF (C AND 192)<>192 THEN . . .

to detect both pumps. In one case, the THEN . . . is executed, while in the other, the next sequential line number is executed, when the condition has been met.

Step 6

In order to test your program steps, add a series of steps to your program so that DANGER is printed when both pumps are on and APPLIANCES when any of the appliances are on. Write your program steps in the following space and review them before you attempt to use them.

Your program steps will probably look like these:

```
120   B = INP(7): C = B
      .
      .
      .
190   GOTO 300
      .
      .
      .
300   IF (C AND 7)=0 THEN 350
310   PRINT@ 576, "APPLIANCES";
320   IF (C AND 192)<>192 THEN 400
330   PRINT@ 640, "DANGER";
340   GOTO 100
350   PRINT@ 576, "        ";
360   GOTO 320
400   PRINT@ 640, "        ";
410   GOTO 100
```

Test your program.

You may have forgotten to add steps to your program that would clear or remove the DANGER and APPLIANCES display, if the conditions were not met. This is easily forgotten. The statements at lines 350 and 400 contain enough spaces to print over APPLIANCES and DANGER, respectively, so that the display is cleared if the conditions are not met.

The program could have been much more complex, containing steps to flash on the screen in case of a danger condition, etc. This experiment should have shown you how flexible the TRS-80 is in tackling control tasks. The software can handle both mathematical and logical operations easily.

You may turn off the computer, but do not remove the input-port interface. It will be used in Experiment No. 9.

EXPERIMENT NO. 8
CONSTRUCTING AN OUTPUT PORT

Purpose

The purpose of the experiment is to have you construct an output port and investigate its use.

Discussion

In this experiment, a simple 8-bit latch circuit will be used to construct an output port. The output port will be used in this experiment, and in some of the following experiments, in which it will be necessary to transfer data to external devices. Two SN7475 quad latch integrated circuits will be used.

Pin Configuration of the Integrated Circuits (Fig. 6-9)

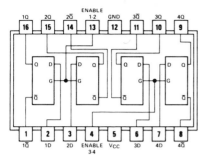

FUNCTION TABLE
(Each Latch)

INPUTS		OUTPUTS	
D	G	Q	Q̄
L	H	L	H
H	H	H	L
X	L	Q_0	$\bar{Q}_0$

H = high level, L = low level, X = irrelevant
Q_0 = the level of Q before the high-to-low transition of G

Fig. 6-9. SN7475 4-bit latch chip pin configuration.

Step 1

The gating circuit used in Experiment No. 2 will be used in this experiment. If this circuit is not available on your solderless breadboard, we suggest that you perform Experiment No. 2 and then this experiment. The circuit may also be wired and used as is. Refer to Fig. 6-4 for circuit details.

Step 2

Wire the circuit shown in Fig. 6-10. Two SN7475 latch integrated circuits are required, along with eight individual lamp monitors. Do not connect the DEV SEL input at present.

Step 3

Refer to the circuit shown in Fig. 6-4. Try to determine which of the SN7402 outputs A, B, or C would be used to control the latch enable inputs. Which would you use? Why?

The A output, IN 7, has already been used and IN 6 would not work since it is decoded for input ports. The OUT 6 output C would be the choice to use. It provides a positive pulse required by the SN7475 latch circuits.

Make a connection between pin 13 on the SN7402 and pin 4 on one of the SN7475 chips. All of the SN7475 enable inputs, G, should be connected in parallel, as shown in Fig. 6-10.

Step 4

To test the output port, enter the following program into the computer:

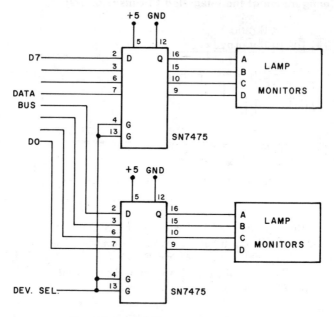

Fig. 6-10. Simple 8-bit output port schematic.

```
10   A = 0
20   OUT 6,A
30   END
```

Preset the variable A to zero, as shown, and run the program. What happens to the lamp monitors?

They should all be unlit. Now set A to 255 and again run the program. You should observe that all of the LEDs at the lamp monitors are lit. If these conditions have not been observed, check your interface wiring for errors.

Step 5

The program may be changed so that values may be input from the keyboard. This new program is

```
10   INPUT A
20   OUT 6,A
30   GOTO 10
```

You may try many different values, but we suggest that you try powers of two first, 0, 1, 2, 4, 8, etc., since these will test the individual LEDs.

Since an 8-bit output port can only display values between zero and 255, what happens when you try to output a value that is outside this range? Would you expect to see a portion of the value? Try using 256 in the program. What do you observe?

The computer displays

?FC ERROR IN 20

which is an Illegal Function Call error message. Thus, the computer will "catch" those attempted transfers in which numbers that are outside of the permitted range are used. Negative numbers will also be "caught."

Step 6

Restart the program and enter a value of 90. You should observe a display of 01011010 on the lamp monitors. Now try and enter a value of − 10. When the error is detected, does the display change?

No. Error conditions are detected prior to the attempted use of the function.

Enter the fractional value 6.001. What is the result displayed on the LEDs?

We observed that the integer portion of the number was displayed. You will observe this for all fractional values. You may wish to experiment with some other values, as well.

Step 7

Can you suggest a short program that could be used to increment a count from zero to 255, and to display it at the output port? Note your program in the following space and test it. What was observed?

We used the following program:

```
10   FOR A = 0 TO 255
20   OUT 6,A
30   NEXT A
40   GOTO 10
```

Remember that you cannot go above the value of 255 for output to port 6. You may wish to introduce a time delay in your program, so that the binary counting may be observed at the least-significant bits; for example,

```
25   FOR I = 1 TO 100: NEXT I
```

The output-port circuit will be used in the following experiment, but the power may be shut off.

EXPERIMENT NO. 9
OUTPUT-PORT AND INPUT-PORT INTERACTIONS

Purpose

The purpose of this experiment is to show how input-port and output-port commands may be used together in a program.

Discussion

In many cases, if input ports and output ports will be used in interfaces. They will be controlled by commands within the same program. In this experiment, you will observe how these I/O ports may be used.

Step 1

The simple input port (Experiment No. 7) and output port (Experiment No. 8) used previously will also be used in this experiment. We refer you to Experiment Nos. 2, 3, and 8 for the appropriate circuit details.

Step 2

Enter the following program into your computer and run it. It is used to test the I/O ports.

```
10   A = INP(7)
20   OUT 6,A
30   GOTO 10
```

As you actuate the logic switches connected to the input port, you should observe that the corresponding LEDs go on, or off, consistent with the switch action. If this is not the case, carefully check your interface.

Step 3

In this step, two values will be entered from the keyboard in succession and then displayed on the LEDs. At this point, you should be able to write a short program to do this. Make an attempt in the following space.

We used the following program, in which a most-significant byte and a least-significant byte were simulated:

```
10  INPUT "MSBY"; Z : M  =  INP(7)
20  INPUT "LSBY"; Z : L  =  INP(7)
30  OUT 6,M
40  INPUT Z
50  OUT 6,L
60  GOTO 10
```

Step 4

Run your program. You should be able to enter two values into the computer, and then have them displayed on "request" at the output port. You may use this program, if you care to do so. Do you observe the desired action? You will have to actuate the ENTER key to have the LSBY displayed.

Step 5

While this short program may be of some use, how could values larger than 255 be displayed at two output ports? How would the values be displayed?

The numbers, between zero and 65,535, for a 16-bit display, would have to be separated into an MSBY and an LSBY. Can you suggest how this might be done?

The number could be divided by 256 to get the MSBY as the integer portion of the answer:

$$10923/256 = 42.668$$

Thus, 42, when converted to binary, would be the MSBY and the LSBY would be

$$10923 - (42 * 256) = 171$$

Thus, the 16-bit representation would be

00101010 10101011

A BASIC program would have to be written to perform these functions. Could you write one?

Step 6

We developed the following program to make the "conversion:"

```
10  INPUT "VALUE"; V
20  M = V/256
30  L = V-FIX(M)*256
40  OUT 6, M
50  INPUT Z
60  OUT 6, L
70  GOTO 10
```

The MSBY will be displayed immediately after the value, V, has been entered. The ENTER key must be depressed to display the LSBY.
Can values greater than 65,535 be entered and converted? Why?

They cannot. Values greater than 65,535, when divided by 256, are greater than 255, the maximum value that may be used with an output command.
What happens to the fractional portion of the result, M, when it is output?

You will probably recall that it is ignored.

EXPERIMENT NO. 10
DATA LOGGING AND DISPLAY

Purpose

The purpose of this experiment is to show you how the input port and output port may be used to acquire information.

Discussion

In this experiment, a list of 10 values will be acquired from the input port, and then displayed on the output port LEDs. More flexible display ideas will also be developed and larger lists acquired.

Step 1

The simple input port and output port used previously will be used in this experiment. We refer you to Experiment Nos. 2, 3, and 8 for the appropriate circuit details.

Step 2

In this experiment, you will acquire and display a set of values that are acquired from the input port. While these may be acquired with software steps such as:

```
50  INPUT Z
60  Q = INP(7)
70  INPUT Z
80  R = INP(7)
    etc.
```

this takes a great number of steps to acquire a small amount of information. Can you suggest an alternative?

A list of values can be acquired through the use of a loop. Can you write a short program that would acquire and display 10 values?

We used the following program, which should look somewhat like yours. Note the use of an array.

```
10   DIM A(10)
20   PRINT "START"
30   FOR I = 1 TO 10
40   INPUT Z
50   A(I) = INP(7)
60   NEXT I
70   PRINT "DISPLAY"
80   FOR I = 1 TO 10
90   INPUT Z
100  OUT 6,A(I)
110  NEXT I
120  GOTO 20
```

In this program, you will have to press ENTER to acquire each value, and when "DISPLAY" is finally displayed, you will have to press ENTER to output each 8-bit value. The actuation of the ENTER key is the synchronizing function between the I/O device and the computer.

Step 3

Run either your program, or our program, to acquire 10 values and to display them. Are the results what you expected?

Yes, the values are stored and then displayed. Eleven values could be acquired, with a simple software modification, since arrays have a zeroeth number.

Step 4

A display of the values on the monitor might be more useful, so devise software steps that could be substituted for the "DISPLAY" steps. Develop your program in the space provided.

We made the following changes in our program:

```
 90   PRINT A(I)
110   NEXT I
120   GOTO 20
```

in which step 100 was removed from the program.

Make a similar change in your program. Run your program. Are the displayed results what you expected?

They should be. All 10 values should be displayed as their decimal equivalents in a column.

Step 5

The graphic-display mode could also be used to display the values that have been acquired. We suggest that you attempt to use the SET command to generate a bar graph for the 10 values. Remember the limits of X and Y for the set command. Note your display program steps in the following space.

We used the following steps to generate such a display:

```
70   CLS
80   FOR I = 1 TO 10
85   M = 47
90   N = 48 - (A(I)*47/256)
100  SET (I,M)
110  IF M<N THEN 130
120  M = M - 1
125  GOTO 100
130  NEXT I
140  END
```

These steps were added to the program that was previously developed. Run either our program, or the one that you have developed. What happens to the display when the program has ended?

The TRS-80 displays

```
READY
>—
```

If this is objectionable, you may replace statement 140 with

```
140  GOTO 140
```

You will have to press BREAK to restart the BASIC interpreter program.

Step 6

Additional changes could be made to the program, so that a time delay was used rather than the INPUT Z statement. This would mean that points would be acquired at regular intervals.

The SN7402 NOR gate circuit shown in Fig. 6-4 should still be wired to your computer. If it is, connect the logic probe input to point "B" at pin 10 on the SN7402. This output, generated by an INP(6) command will be used as a visual signal for the end of a time delay. The logic probe should be connected solely to the SN7402.

How would you modify the program to use a time delay in place of the INPUT Z command? How would you modify the program so that 25 values are obtained, rather than 10? Show your program steps in the following space.

We modified the following steps:

```
10   DIM A(25)
     .
     .
     .
30   FOR I = 1 TO 25
40   FOR Q = 1 TO 750: NEXT Q: Q = INP(6)
     .
     .
     .
80   FOR I = 1 TO 25
```

Note that the commands at line 40 generate a time delay, and also pulse the logic probe, indicating that the next value is to be acquired.

You have probably noticed that not all of the changes in your switch settings were shown on the bar graph. Do you know why?

The values of zero to 255 are represented in 47 steps. Each step, therefore, represents a larger difference in the displayed values than can be affected by a step from zero to one, for example. The display has less resolution than the 8-bit input port. The one-part-in-256 value from the input port is now displayed as one part in 47. Therefore, some resolution is lost in our bar graph.

EXPERIMENT NO. 11
SIMPLE DIGITAL-TO-ANALOG CONVERTER

Purpose

The purpose of this experiment is to show you how a simple 8-bit digital-to-analog converter (D/A or DAC) can be interfaced to the TRS-80.

Discussion

A simple D/A converter, the Signetics NE5018 8-bit converter, will be interfaced to the TRS-80. Although we have not discussed D/A converters, they have been covered in *Microcomputer-Analog Converter Software and Hardware Interfacing* (Howard W. Sams & Co., Inc., Indianapolis, IN 46206). We refer you to this book for additional information about D/A converters. Other topics such as sample and holds, analog multiplexers and instrumentation amplifiers are also covered in this book.

Pin Configuration of the Integrated Circuit (Fig. 6-11)

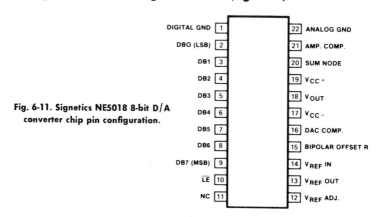

Fig. 6-11. Signetics NE5018 8-bit D/A converter chip pin configuration.

Step 1

Two additional power supplies are required in this experiment, +12 and −12 volts. They will be used to power the D/A converter. Be sure that these power supplies are available before proceeding.

Wire the circuit shown in Fig. 6-12. The device-select pulse is obtained from the SN7402 circuit that was wired in Experiment No. 2, Fig. 6-4. The device select is available from point "C," but it must be inverted, using an SN7404 or equivalent inverter function. This is shown in Fig. 6-13.

Step 2

The NE5018 interface will convert values between 0 and 255 to voltages of between zero and +10 volts. Since the 0- to 10-volt range has been divided into 256 values, or 255 steps, the voltage increment available is 39 millivolts per step.

Could you write a program that would increment the count pre-

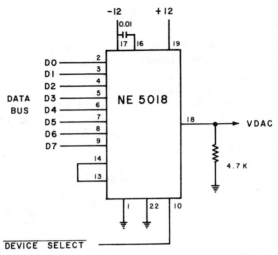

Fig. 6-12. Schematic for simple D/A converter interface, using NE5018 D/A converter chip.

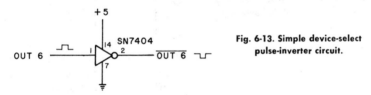

Fig. 6-13. Simple device-select pulse-inverter circuit.

sented to the D/A converter to generate a positive ramp, or a slowly increasing voltage? Develop your program steps in the space below:

We used the following program:

```
10  FOR I = 0 TO 255
20  OUT 6,I
30  NEXT I
40  GOTO 10
```

A simple voltmeter or volt-ohm-milliammeter (vom) may be used to monitor the voltages. Connect the meter between ground and the NE5018 VDAC output. Try your program. Does the voltage increase slowly? What happens when it reaches 10 volts?

The voltage ramps slowly up to 10 volts. When it reaches this value, it quickly changes to ground, or zero volts. You should also be able to develop a program that produces a negative ramp and possibly even a triangular waveform.

Step 3

Develop a program that will generate a negative ramp, and also a program that will generate a triangular output.

We used the following programs:

```
10   FOR I = 255 TO 0  STEP-1
20   OUT 6,I
30   NEXT I
40   GOTO 10
```

```
10   FOR I = 0 TO 255
20   OUT 6,I
30   NEXT I
40   FOR I = 254 TO 1  STEP-1
50   OUT 6,I
60   NEXT I
70   GOTO 10
```

You may wish to try either of these programs, or the ones you have developed. Why is the "range" in the loop command at statement 40 not 0 TO 255?

If the "range" was 0 TO 255, the values of zero and 255 would be output twice.

Step 4

Since you know that the voltage of zero to 10 volts corresponds to steps from zero to 255, can you develop a program that would allow you to enter an actual voltage setting from the keyboard and that would generate this voltage on the meter? Use the following space for your program.

We developed the following program.

```
10   INPUT "VOLTAGE"; V
20   I = V*25.5
30   OUT 6,I
40   GOTO 10
```

Step 5

Try your program. Does it generate a voltage from the D/A converter that closely matches the value that you entered into the TRS-80? Our program seemed to work well.

Step 6

At this point, you should be able to write a program that allows you to enter a lower- and an upper-limit for voltages in a triangular waveform. Develop your program in the space provided.

We used the following program to do this.

```
10    INPUT "HI V"; H
20    INPUT "LO V"; L
30    H = H*25.5
40    L = L*25.5
50    FOR I = L TO H
60    OUT 6,I
70    NEXT I
80    HA = H-1 : LA = L+1
90    FOR I = HA TO LA   STEP-1
100   OUT 6,I
110   NEXT I
120   GOTO 50
```

Run your program and test it. You should be able to make the meter needle "swing" between the two voltages that you have preset.

This experiment should clearly illustrate the use of D/A converters, and the power of BASIC in controlling them.

You may disassemble your interface and turn off your computer.

EXPERIMENT NO. 12
DEVICE ADDRESS-DECODER CIRCUITS

Purpose

The purpose of this experiment is to have you learn about the construction of device address-decoder circuits.

Discussion

In many cases, you may want to develop your own interface circuits that do not use the breadboard. The device address-decoders used to identify individual I/O devices must be constructed using standard SN7400-series integrated circuits. In this experiment, you will construct two decoder circuits. Since address bits A3-A0 are the only ones readily available for experimental use, the decoders that you will construct will be nonabsolutely decoded.

Pin Configuration of the Integrated Circuits (Fig. 6-14)

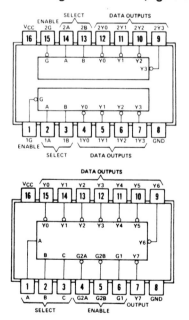

Fig. 6-14. SN74LS138 and SN74LS139 decoder chip pin configurations.

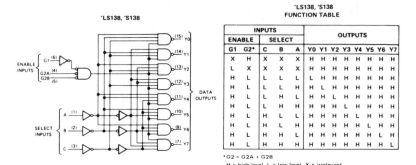

'LS138, 'S138

'LS138, 'S138
FUNCTION TABLE

INPUTS					OUTPUTS							
ENABLE		SELECT										
G1	G2*	C	B	A	Y0	Y1	Y2	Y3	Y4	Y5	Y6	Y7
X	H	X	X	X	H	H	H	H	H	H	H	H
L	X	X	X	X	H	H	H	H	H	H	H	H
H	L	L	L	L	L	H	H	H	H	H	H	H
H	L	L	L	H	H	L	H	H	H	H	H	H
H	L	L	H	L	H	H	L	H	H	H	H	H
H	L	L	H	H	H	H	H	L	H	H	H	H
H	L	H	L	L	H	H	H	H	L	H	H	H
H	L	H	L	H	H	H	H	H	H	L	H	H
H	L	H	H	L	H	H	H	H	H	H	L	H
H	L	H	H	H	H	H	H	H	H	H	H	L

*G2 = G2A + G2B
H = high level, L = low level, X = irrelevant

Fig. 6-15. SN74LS138 decoder schematic and function table.

The schematic diagrams and function tables for both of these decoders are provided in Figs. 6-15 and 6-16.

Step 1

Wire the circuit shown in Fig. 6-17. The address outputs are present on the 8-pin socket that also makes the connection with the logic probe. What addresses would be decoded in this circuit?

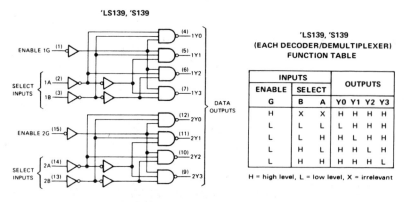

'LS139, 'S139

'LS139, 'S139
(EACH DECODER/DEMULTIPLEXER)
FUNCTION TABLE

INPUTS			OUTPUTS			
ENABLE	SELECT					
G	B	A	Y0	Y1	Y2	Y3
H	X	X	H	H	H	H
L	L	L	L	H	H	H
L	L	H	H	L	H	H
L	H	L	H	H	L	H
L	H	H	H	H	H	L

H = high level, L = low level, X = irrelevant

Fig. 6-16. SN74LS139 decoder schematic and function table.

Actually, none. The gating inputs must be properly connected to logic one or logic zero for the decoder to operate properly. How would you connect these inputs to cause the decoder to operate properly?

Fig. 6-17. SN74LS138 decoder circuit schematic.

You should connect G1 to logic one and G2A and G2B to ground.

Step 2

Connect the decoder input G1 to logic one (+5V) and inputs G2A and G2B to ground. Connect power to your system, and start the computer. You should now be able to observe the presence of logic levels on the eight outputs, Y0-Y7. Why are these changing levels present? What addresses is the decoder selecting?

The pulse, or logic-level activity, is observed as a normal part of the computer operation. The decoder is decoding addresses XXXXXXXX XXXXX000 through XXXXXXXX XXXXX111.

Step 3

A NOR gate could be used to combine the function pulses $\overline{\text{IN}}$ or $\overline{\text{OUT}}$ with the various decoded outputs for device selection. To select all of the eight output device select signals, eight NOR gates, or two SN7402 (or equivalent) integrated circuits would be required. Can you suggest a means of gating the device address *and* the function pulse, $\overline{\text{OUT}}$, right in the SN74LS138 chip?

Either of the G2 inputs could be connected to the $\overline{\text{OUT}}$ signal, instead of being grounded. There are two zero input gating signals. Could one be used for $\overline{\text{OUT}}$ and the other for $\overline{\text{IN}}$?

No, since they are never logic zero at the same time, a requirement for the operation of the SN74LS138.

Step 4

Remove the connection between the G2A pin (pin 4) and ground (logic zero) of the SN74LS138. Connect this pin to the $\overline{\text{OUT}}$ signal at the CONTROL SIGNALS socket. With the computer now running, do you observe any pulses at the light outputs of the decoder?

With no program running, but with the TRS-80 in the READY mode, we did not observe any outputs, other than logic ones, at the decoder outputs.

Write a short program that will pulse the Y5 output of the decoder. What is the address that will activate this output?

We used the following program:

```
10   OUT 5,0
20   GOTO 10
```

The address we selected was 5, or 00000101. Would any other addresses actuate this output? What are they?

There are 32 different addresses that could be used; XXXXX101 where X = 1 or 0. Examples are 5, 13, 21, 29, etc., through 253. Remember, this decoder is not absolutely decoding all of the address bits.

Step 5

Likewise, the $\overline{\text{IN}}$ pulse could be substituted for the $\overline{\text{OUT}}$ pulse to generate eight device-select pulses for input devices. Could the decoder scheme be configured so that address bit A3 could also be used? How could this be readily accomplished?

Address bit A3 could be used as an additional gating signal, at either input G1, or at input G2B, depending on whether we want the decoder active when A3 = logic one, or when A3 = logic zero.

Remove the wire between the decoder G1 input (pin 6) and the +5-volt supply, or other logic one connection. Now, connect address bit A3 to pin 6 on the SN74LS138 decoder. What addresses will now be decoded?

Addresses XXXX1000 through XXXX1111 will be decoded, or addresses 8 through 15.

Step 6

Write a short program that will pulse the Y3 output of the decoder. What device address have you chosen?

We used the following program:

```
10  OUT 251,0
20  GOTO 10
```

and we chose address 251, since in its binary representation, it is 11111011, the equivalent of XXXX1011. Change your program so that you can test some of the other outputs of the decoder. We used the following short program:

```
10  INPUT I
20  OUT I,0
30  GOTO 10
```

Step 7

Now change your circuit so that the decoder is only functional when address bit A3 is a logic zero, and when the $\overline{OUT}$ pulse is present. Test your changes by running a short program, such as the one in Step 6, to exercise the various output-port addresses.

You should have the A3 address signal connected to the G2B input (pin 5), with the decoder pin 6 connected to logic one.

Step 8

If you have a number of SN74LS138 decoders available, how many device-select pulses can you generate, using circuits such as those that you have developed so far? You may wish to sketch some simple circuits, Assume that only address lines A3-A0 are available.

You should be able to generate 16 output-port device-select pulses, and 16 input-port device-select pulses, too. This requires the use of four SN74LS138 decoders. Likewise, two SN74154 or SN74 LS154 decoders could have been used, as discussed in the text portion of the book.

For absolute decoding, bits A7-A4, on the address bus, would also have to be decoded in some way to further gate the SN74LS138 decoders. This is shown in Fig. 6-18. In this circuit, device addresses 11110000 through 11111111 have been decoded for both input and output devices.

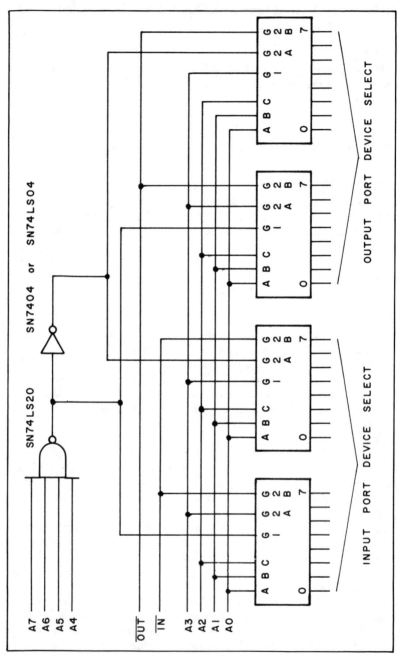

Fig. 6-18. Absolute decoder circuit schematic using SN74LS138 decoder.

Step 9

Some computer systems do not require a large number of I/O port device-select pulses. In this type of a situation, the SN74LS139 dual two-line to four-line decoder is quite useful. It is shown in Figs. 6-14 and 6-17. Since two independent decoders have been provided, separate input-port and output-port device-select pulses may be generated.

Step 10

Wire the circuit shown in Fig. 6-19. Using the logic probe, check all eight outputs. Are any active? Be sure that the computer is on, but that it is not running a BASIC program. Are these results what you would expect?

We observed that all of the outputs were in the logic one state. Since no INP or OUT commands are being executed, this is what we would expect.

Step 11

Write a short program that would pulse the $\overline{\text{IN 3}}$ device select output and the $\overline{\text{OUT 1}}$ device select output. Confirm the proper operation of the decoder.

We used the following program:

```
10  A = INP(3)
20  OUT 1,A
30  GOTO 10
```

The pulses were observed at pins 7 and 11 on the SN74LS139 chip.
What device addresses will activate this decoder?

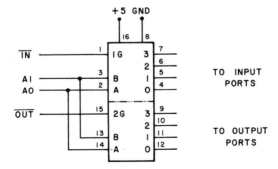

Fig. 6-19. SN74LS139 used for I/O port device-select pulse generation.

The device addresses of XXXXXX00 through XXXXXX11 may be used with either INP or OUT commands.

Remember, this simple decoder scheme is not absolutely decoded. It is more difficult to add additional decoders to the circuits that use the SN74LS139 decoders than it is to add such additional decoders to the circuits that use the SN74LS138 decoder.

While these circuits may be useful in some applications, and for testing interfaces during breadboarding, we recommend the use of absolute addressing schemes whenever possible.

EXPERIMENT NO. 13
OUTPUT PORTS, BCD, AND BINARY CODES

Purpose

The purpose of this experiment is to explore the use of the SN74LS373 octal-latch circuit as an output port.

Discussion

Newer integrated circuits, such as the SN74LS373 octal latch, are available to simplify the task of output-port construction. In this experiment, the SN74LS373 will be used, and its three-state output capability will also be demonstrated.

Pin Configuration of the Integrated Circuit (Fig. 6-20)

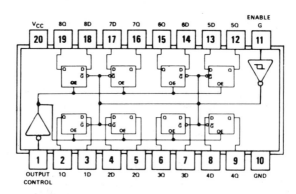

Fig. 6-20. SN74LS373 octal latch chip pin configuration.

Step 1

Wire the circuit shown in Fig. 6-21. An SN7402 or SN74LS02 NOR-gate integrated circuit is also required. At this point, you should be able to wire the NOR gate without assistance. You may wish to refer to Fig. 6-5 for the SN7402 pin configuration.

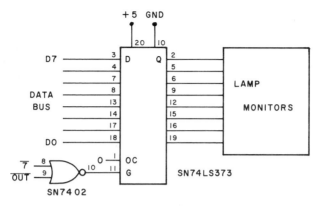

Fig. 6-21. Using SN74LS373 octal latch chip as output port.

Step 2

Note that the SN74LS373 octal latch has two control inputs. One controls the latch, while the other controls the latch outputs. These outputs may be in either the data state, passing the latched information through to the outputs, or they may be in the high-impedance, or disconnected, third state. This relationship is shown in Table 6-3.

Table 6-3. Control Signal Truth Table for the SN74LS373

Output Control	Enable (G)	Data	Output
L	H	H	H
L	H	L	L
L	L	X	Q_0
H	X	X	Z

When the Output Control signal is a logic one, the outputs have been disabled, or placed in the high-impedance third state (Z). When the Enable input, G, is a logic one, the information is passed through the latch, as was the case for the SN7475 latch chips.

You should be able to connect the Output Control input (OC) on the SN74LS373 chip to ground so that the outputs are enabled at all times.

Step 3

Once the output port has been wired, test it by writing a short program that will exercise the various outputs.

We used a program that incremented the lamp monitor display, and also a program that allowed us to enter a value and then observe its binary equivalent at the output port. You should not need any additional assistance to do this.

Step 4

Load the following program into your computer and run it.

```
10   FOR I = 0 TO 255
20   OUT 7,I
30   FOR T = 1 TO 300 : NEXT T
40   NEXT I
50   GOTO 10
```

What do you observe at the lamp monitors?

You should observe a slowly incrementing binary count.

Now that the display is "counting," carefully remove the connection between the SN74LS373 Output Control pin (pin 1) and ground. What happens to the display? When you replace this connection, what is observed on the display?

In our display, all of the lamp monitors became unlit. When the Output Control was again grounded, the count was observed to be continuing. *The Output Control did not affect the count.* The Output Control placed the latch outputs in the high-impedance state. In our system, this caused the lamp monitors to turn off.

Step 5

In this step, the three-state capability of the SN74LS373 latch will be used, so that two latch chips may share a common 8-bit display.

With the breadboard power disconnected, wire a second SN74-LS373 latch circuit in parallel [all inputs wired to the data bus, all outputs (D7 to D7, D3 to D3) wired together] with the one already wired. *Do not make parallel connections between the Output Control pins (pin 1) or the Enable inputs (pins 11).* Place both of the Output Enable pins in the logic one state, by connecting them to +5 volts.

A second NOR gate will be required to control the second latch. You can wire the NOR gate as shown in Fig. 6-22. This schematic diagram also shows an optional NOR-gate circuit that may be used to alternate between the selection of the outputs of one or the other SN74LS373 latches. When the NOR-gate inputs (pins 3 and 2) are grounded, output port 6 will have its 8-bit value displayed, while output port 7 will have its value displayed when the NOR gate pins 3 and 2 are at +5 volts or logic one. If you decide to use the optional

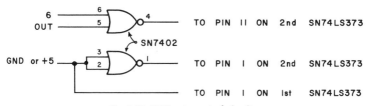

Fig. 6-22. NOR-gate control circuit.

lower NOR-gate circuit, remember to remove the connections between +5 volts and pin 1 on each SN74LS373. We recommend the use of the NOR-gate circuit. This circuit should only be wired to the SN74LS373s with the power off.

Step 6

At this point, you may wish to test output port 6. If you do so, remember to enable it, and to disable port 7. They must not be enabled at the same time. You should be able to test the output port without further assistance.

You should be able to write a program that will increment a 16-bit count, displaying the count on the two latch outputs. (You will have to enable the outputs of the appropriate latch to see the count.) Write your program and test it.

We used the following program:

```
1000   For B = 0 TO 255
1010   FOR C = 0 TO 255
1020   OUT 7,C
1030   OUT 6,B
1040   NEXT C
1050   NEXT B
1060   GOTO 1000
```

Remember that the OUT commands can only accept values between zero and 255.

Step 7

In the previous step, the computer counted in binary. One additional code, frequently used by counters, displays, and digital instruments, is the binary coded decimal or bcd code. This code is binary, too, since it uses ones and zeros, but it encodes decimal digits, one digit at a time. Thus 9530 becomes 1001 0101 0011 0000 when converted to bcd. If you are not familiar with the bcd coding, you may wish to obtain some more information before going further.

In this step, you will develop a computer program that will convert values between zero and 9999 to their equivalent bcd values. Thus, if the value 5367 was keyed into the TRS-80, you should see the "53" or 01010011 displayed at output port 6, while the "67" is displayed at output port 7.

We used the following program to perform the conversions:

```
10   INPUT "VALUE ="; A
20   IF A < 10000 THEN 30   ELSE 10
30   GOSUB 1000
40   OUT 7,A+C
50   A = B
60   GOSUB 1000
70   OUT 6,A+C
80   GOTO 10

1000 B = 0 : C = 0
1010 IF A > 99   THEN 1100
1020 IF A < 10   THEN RETURN
1030 C = C+16 : A = A−10
1040 GOTO 1020
1100 A = A−100 : B = B+1
1110 GOTO 1010
```

In the subroutine, the variables are A, B, and C. In this case, the A represents the decimal value to be converted to bcd (the starting value), B represents the "hundreds," while C represents the "tens." At the end of the subroutine, the A value represents the units.

In some cases, it may be difficult for you to remember that we are tricking the TRS-80 into generating bcd values for us. In most cases, four seven-segment (or equivalent) displays would be used for the actual display. In this case, we economized, and used one

8-bit display, along with the three-state output capability of the SN74LS373 latch.

If you plan to go on to the next experiment, do not disturb your circuit, although one output port (port 6) may be removed.

EXPERIMENT NO. 14
OUTPUT-PORTS TRAFFIC-LIGHT CONTROLLER

Purpose

The purpose of this experiment is to show you how the TRS-80 may be used as a controller in a real application.

Discussion

While the control of a traffic light may not seem like a realistic problem for us to tackle with the computer, it does illustrate the ability of the computer to make decisions and control external events.

Step 1

An 8-bit output port will be used in this experiment. If you have one already constructed, you may use it as long as it can control some LEDs. If you have completed Experiment No. 13, you may use Output port 7. Output port 6 may be removed.

If you need to construct an output port, we refer you to Experiment No. 13, Figs. 6-20 and 6-21.

Lamp monitors or individual LEDs may be used to simulate the positions of the traffic light, but only six are required, since the north-south and east-west lamps would be the same, with a red, yellow, and green lamp for each. We used colored LEDs and we adopted the following convention.

BIT	LED		BIT	LED	
D0	RED	}	D3	RED	}
D1	YELLOW	} ELM	D4	YELLOW	} MAIN
D2	GREEN	}	D5	GREEN	}

Step 2

You must now determine the patterns of logic ones and zeros that are required to turn of the individual LEDs. Since our circuit could drive the LEDs directly, logic zeros turned the LEDs on in our "traffic light." What values are to be output to port 7 to turn the various lights on and off?

We found that the following values were needed:

ELM	Red	254_{10}	11111110_2	MAIN	Red	247_{10}	11110111_2
ELM	Yellow	235	11111101	MAIN	Yellow	239	11101111
ELM	Green	251	11111011	MAIN	Green	223	11011111

Step 3

To start the traffic-light control, write a program that will flash the yellow light on Main Street and the red light on Elm Street; one second on and one second off. Use a general-purpose one-second delay statement. What is the "on" pattern, and what is the "off" pattern?

The off pattern is 255, or all logic ones, while the on pattern has bits D4 and D0 both as logic zeros, or 238_{10}. We used the following program:

```
10   OUT 7,255
20   FOR T = 1 TO 300 : NEXT T
30   OUT 7,238
40   FOR T = 1 TO 300 : NEXT T
50   GOTO 10
```

Step 4

Determine the lamp patterns that will be required for normal traffic-light operation. What are they? How can they be stored in the computer?

The patterns are a) red on Elm, green on Main (222), b) red on Elm, yellow on Main (238), c) green on Elm, red on Main (243), and d) yellow on Elm, red on Main (245). The values could be stored through the use of DATA statements, subscripted variables, or just as variables, one per lamp pattern.

Step 5

In the remainder of this experiment, we will assume a "yellow period" of two seconds. Thus, if Elm Street is on a 10-second period, the green light will be on for 10 seconds, followed by a 2-second yellow, before the red signal comes on.

Write a program that will allow you to sequence through the light patterns, with a 6-second period on Elm and a 10-second period on Main Street.

We used the following program:

```
10    M = 10: E = 6
20    DATA 222, 238, 243, 245
30    READ L
40    OUT 7,L
50    FOR I = 0 TO M
60    FOR T = 1 TO 300 : NEXT T
70    NEXT I
80    READ L
90    OUT 7,L
100   GOSUB 1000
110   READ L
120   OUT 7,L
130   FOR I = 0 TO E
140   FOR T = 1 TO 300 : NEXT T
150   NEXT I
160   READ L
170   OUT 7,L
180   GOSUB 1000
190   RESTORE
200   GOTO 30

1000  FOR I = 0 TO 2
1010  FOR T = 1 TO 300 : NEXT T
1020  NEXT I
1030  RETURN
```

Step 6

While the program listed in the previous step will operate correctly, many of the steps are repetitive. Could you suggest a new program that could be written in a simpler way? How would you simplify it?

In the program in Step 5, the only changes are made in each of the major steps in the program are the light patterns and the time delay. By using an array of values, one simple loop may be used.

We found that the following program worked well:

```
 10   A(1) = 222: A(2) = 238: A(3) = 243: A(4) = 245
 20   M(1) = 0: M(2) = 2: M(3) = 0: M(4) = 2
 30   INPUT "MAIN"; M(1)
 40   INPUT "ELM"; M(3)
 50   FOR Q = 1 TO 4
 60   OUT 7,A(Q)
 70   FOR I = 0 TO M(Q)
 80   FOR T = 1 TO 300 : NEXT T
 90   NEXT I
100   NEXT Q
110   GOTO 50
```

In this new program, the A array stores the light patterns, while the M array stores the time intervals.

Step 7

So far, the computer has only served as a sequencer, generating the proper time delays and traffic-light codes. In this step, some control functions will be added to the traffic-light program.

The traffic on Main Street is usually heavy, so the normal mode should be green on Main and red on Elm. The program should be able to detect a single car waiting on Elm Street, so that it may be given the green light. The Elm Street green sequence should take place only after 30 seconds of Main Street green have elapsed.

In order to program this, you will probably wish to draw a flowchart of the program. The keyboard E and M keys may be used as the "street sensors" on Elm and Main streets, respectively. You may wish to shorten the periods so that the program may be tested quickly.

We used approximately 10-second delay periods with 2-second "yellow periods." The program we used is

```
 10   A = 0
 15   REM RED ON ELM, GREEN ON MAIN
 20   OUT 7,222
 30   FOR I = 0 TO 10
 40   FOR T = 0 TO 300 : NEXT T
 50   NEXT I
 60   A$ = INKEY$
 65   REM E KEY PRESSED AFTER 10 SECONDS
 70   IF A$ = "E"  THEN 80   ELSE 60
 75   REM RED ON ELM, YELLOW ON MAIN
 80   OUT 7,238
 90   FOR I = 0 TO 2
100   FOR T = 0 TO 300 : NEXT T
110   NEXT I
```

```
115   REM GREEN ON ELM, RED ON MAIN
120   OUT 7,243
130   FOR I = 0 TO 10
140   FOR T = 0 TO 150
150   B$ = INKEY$
160   IF B$ = "M" THEN 190
170   NEXT T : NEXT I
180   GOTO 210
190   A = A+1
200   IF A = 5 THEN 210 ELSE 170
205   REM YELLOW ON ELM, RED ON MAIN
210   OUT 7,245
220   FOR I = 0 TO 2
230   FOR T = 0 TO 300 : NEXT T
240   NEXT I
250   GOTO 10
```

You should note that when the green light is present on Elm Street, the keyboard key-detecting steps are embedded in the time-delay steps. Thus, these steps become part of the delay steps. Also, you may note that even if the E key is actuated *once* during the initial 30-second delay period, the E key will be sensed at the end of the delay. Apparently, the BASIC program stores the last pressed key and uses this in the A$ = INKEY$ step.

What does the M key do? It aborts the Elm Street green period if 5 cars are detected on Main Street. Many other routines could be added, for multiple sensors, advanced turn lanes, pedestrian cross-walks, etc.

The six LEDs should be removed and the power may be turned off. An output port will be used in the next experiment, so you should leave the one used in this experiment intact.

EXPERIMENT NO. 15
LOGIC-DEVICE TESTER

Purpose

The purpose of this experiment is to show you how the computer may be used to test logic devices for proper operation.

Discussion

Most logic "chips" that contain gates may be tested by applying known logic-level inputs to the gate inputs, and then comparing the gate output with a truth table for the type of device being tested. In this experiment, the computer will be used in such a manner. One input port, and one output port are required. Various devices such as SN7400, SN7402, SN7408, etc., may be tested. The test is a functional test, and not a test for dynamic properties, such as switching time, propagation, delay, and other parameters.

Step 1

You will need to construct an input port and an output port. You should be able to do this without further assistance. Many of the previous experiments have detailed this. You may wish to use an SN74LS373 chip as the 8-bit input port. When these ports have been constructed, go on to the next step.

Step 2

The test configuration for an SN7400 NAND-gate package is shown in Fig. 6-23. For the pin configurations of other gate circuits we refer you to Fig. 6-24.

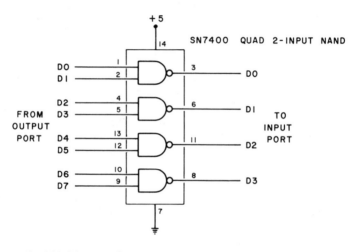

Fig. 6-23. Schematic of circuit used to test SN7400 NAND-gate chips under computer control.

Wire the test circuit shown in Fig. 6-23. Remember to connect the +5-volt and ground-power inputs to both the interface chips and the integrated circuit being tested.

You should be able to develop the truth tables for various gates, starting with the NAND gate. For a two-input gate, there are only four combinations of inputs. How many different combinations would there be for the four gates in the SN7400 package?

Possibly you said 16 combinations, four for each gate, or 256 combinations, the number possible with eight output lines to the eight inputs in the package. Actually there are still only four combinations, since all gates are tested at the same time. Knowing that one gate is bad means that the entire package is bad.

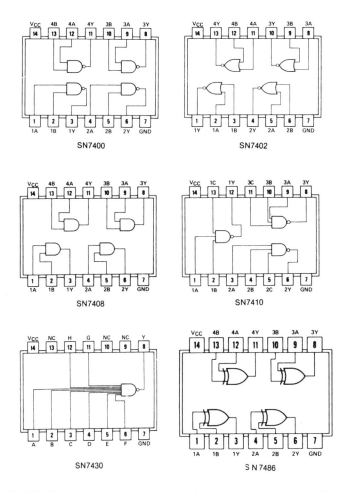

Fig. 6-24. Pin configurations of some standard SN7400-series chips that readily test under computer control.

Step 3

What are the four combinations that will be used at the output port? You should develop both binary and decimal values.

Our values were:

00	00	00	00	= 0
01	01	01	01	= 85
10	10	10	10	= 170
11	11	11	11	= 255

Since the outputs have been connected to input bits D3-D0, we would expect the gate outputs to be all zeros or all ones; 0 or 15, as a result. Since all of the gates are tested at once, the results should be the same for all gates.

How could the bits input at positions D7-D4 be eliminated from the test?

These could be set to zero by a logic AND operation with the mask 00001111.

Step 4

Develop a short program that will test the NAND gate that you have interfaced. Your program may closely resemble the traffic-light control program shown in Experiment No. 14, Step 6. The program does not have to be very complex.

The following program worked quite well in this application:

```
10   T(1) = 0: T(2) = 85: T(3) = 170: T(4) = 255
20   R(1) = 15: R(2) = 15: R(3) = 15: R(4) = 0
30   FOR I = 1 TO 4
40   OUT 7,T(I)
50   IF (15 AND INP(6)) = R(I) THEN 60 ELSE 100
60   NEXT I
70   CLS: PRINT@ 128, "TEST OK": END
100  CLS: PRINT@ 128, "FAILURE": END
```

Step 5

Since the pin configurations for the SN7400, SN7408, and SN7486 are equivalent, could a generalized test program be developed for them? How?

Yes, a general-test program would be possible. The user could enter the device name and the computer would select the truth-table information to be used. The truth tables are shown in Table 6-4.

Table 6-4. Truth Tables for the NAND, AND, and EXOR Gates

SN7400			SN7408			SN7486		
A	B	OUT	A	B	OUT	A	B	OUT
0	0	1	0	0	0	0	0	0
0	1	1	0	1	0	0	1	1
1	0	1	1	0	0	1	0	1
1	1	0	1	1	1	1	1	0

You should note that the test patterns are the same, only the results change.

We used the following program:

```
10   INPUT "LAST TWO DIGITS"; G
20   IF G = 0 THEN 200
30   IF G = 8 THEN 300
40   IF G = 86 THEN 400
50   PRINT "TEST NOT AVAILABLE": GOTO 10
60   T(1) = 0: T(2) = 85: T(3) = 170: T(4) = 255
70   FOR I = 1 TO 4
80   OUT 7,T(I)
90   IF(15 AND INP(6)) = R(I) THEN 100 ELSE 140
100  NEXT I
110  CLS: PRINT@ 128, "TEST OK": END
140  CLS: PRINT@ 128, "FAILURE": END

200  R(1) = 15: R(2) = 15: R(3) = 15: R(4) = 0
210  GOTO 60
300  R(1) = 0: R(2) = 0: R(3) = 0: R(4) = 15
310  GOTO 60
400  R(1) = 0: R(2) = 15: R(3) = 15: R(4) = 0
410  GOTO 60
```

The last two digits requested are the last two digits in the device number; that is, 00 for SN7400, 08 for SN7408 and 86 for SN7486. If several SN7400, SN7408 and SN7486 chips are available, you may wish to test these using the program listed in this step.

Step 6

It should also be possible for the computer to test logic devices such as counters and flip-flops. If you are familiar with the SN7493 4-bit binary counter, you may wish to try the following steps. If not, you may wish to read through these steps.

The pin configuration and schematic diagram of the SN7493 counter is provided in Fig. 6-25. In order to test this device, the counter outputs must be available to the computer, and the computer must be able to clock and reset the counter, independently. We will not test the counter exhaustively, but we will test the reset and counting ability.

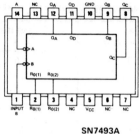

Fig. 6-25. SN7493 4-bit counter
pin configuration.

SN7493A
SN74LS93

Step 7

Wire the SN7493 counter as shown in Fig. 6-26. You will need an input port and two SN7402 (SN74LS02 or SN74L02) NOR gates, as well as the SN7493 that is to be tested. (DO NOT USE AN SN74L93.)

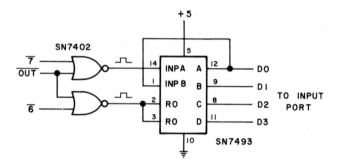

Fig. 6-26. Test circuit schematic used to check SN7493 4-bit counter chips.

Step 8

Write a short test program that will exercise the reset function and the counting function. Do not try to write a very complex program at this time.

We used the following program:

```
10   OUT 5,0
20   IF (15 AND INP(6)) > 0 THEN 1000
30   CLS: PRINT@ 64, "RESET TEST OK"
```

```
  40   FOR I = 1 TO 15
  50   OUT 7,0
  60   IF (15 AND INP(6)) = I THEN 70 ELSE 1100
  70   NEXT I
  80   PRINT@ 128, "COUNT TEST OK": END
1000   CLS: PRINT@ 64, "RESET FAILURE": END
1100   PRINT@ 128, "COUNT FAILURE", I: END
```

The program first tests the reset and then the count. If a counting failure occurs, the count expected is printed in the failure message. This program again uses the logical AND operation to mask bits D7-D4.

Step 9

The program does not test all 16-counter states. The last count, from 1111 to 0000 is not tested. Could you modify the program so that this test is made? Try to do so.

We substituted the following new steps in the program:

```
  40   FOR I = 1 TO 16
```

and

```
  60   IF (15 AND INP(6)) = (15 AND I) THEN 70 ELSE 1100
```

The additional AND operation in line 60 masks bits D7-D4 in the value I, so that the value seems to go from 15 to zero, or 1111 to 0000, as expected for a 4-bit counter.

The input port should be left on your breadboard. The output port and the program are not required in the following experiments.

EXPERIMENT NO. 16
SIMPLE FLAG CIRCUITS

Purpose

The purpose of this experiment is to demonstrate the construction and use of simple flag circuits.

Discussion

Flags are signals that are used by the computer so that the computer and I/O device operations are synchronized. Flags are used to indicate busy/ready, full/empty, on/off, and other combinations to the computer. Experiment No. 6 illustrated the use of input ports for nonnumeric information. This experiment will develop this concept further. You will require an input port in this experiment.

Pin Configurations of the Integrated Circuits (Fig. 6-27)

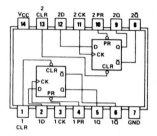

Fig. 6-27. SN7474 dual D-type flip-flop
chip pin configuration.

Step 1

An input port will be required in this experiment. You should be able to construct an input port without further instructions. Many of the past experiments have detailed the construction of these ports, so you should not require any further assistance. Once an input port has been constructed, go on to the next step.

Step 2

One of the previous experiments investigated the use of simple switches as flag inputs. This experiment will explore the use of flip-flops for flag circuits. An SN7474 flip-flop will be used. Wire the circuit shown in Fig. 6-28.

A jumper wire should be used between the clear input, pin 1, and +5 volts, so that the flag may be cleared by a momentary connection between pin 1 and ground, once the jumper has been removed from the +5-volt connection. The pulser circuit may be a pair of

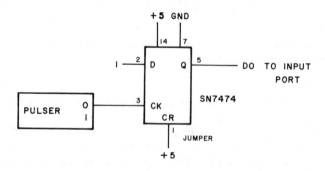

Fig. 6-28. Simple flip-flop–based flag circuit schematic.

cross-coupled NAND gates, or an equivalent circuit that will generate "clean" noise-free logic transitions. This is described in the introduction to the experiments, and the appendix.

Step 3

Once the flag circuit has been wired, enter and run the following program. It is used to test the flag circuit.

```
10  CLS
20  IF (1 AND INP(6)) = 0 THEN 30 ELSE 50
30  PRINT@ 200, "0"
40  GOTO 20
50  PRINT@ 200, "1"
60  GOTO 20
```

When the flag has been cleared (ground the clear pin), the display should show a zero. When the flag is set (the pulser actuated), the display should change to a one. When this works properly, go on to the next step.

Step 4

In this step, the computer will keep track of the number of pulser actuations that have been sensed by the flag. Note the use of the AND operation to mask bits D7-D1, leaving only the flag bit, D0 for the decision-making step. You may wish to use an additional pulser circuit for the flag clearing operation.

Enter the following program and run it:

```
10  CLS: B = 0 : PRINT@ 200, B
20  IF (1 AND INP(6)) = 0 THEN 20 ELSE 30
30  B = B + 1
40  PRINT@ 200, B
50  GOTO 20
```

Be sure that the flip-flop has been cleared before you start the program. With the program running, actuate the pulser to set the flag flip-flop. What do you observe? Is this what you expect? We found that the count started as soon as the push button was pressed, and that it continued until the flag was cleared. This is not what we wanted to do. We wanted one count, each time the pulser was actuated.

Why didn't this happen the way we expected?

The set state of the flag continued to be detected by the program. We could not reset it fast enough by hand to stop the counting at one per pulser actuation.

Step 5

In most computer systems, the computer, or the flag-containing device clears the flag after it has been detected. To allow your

Fig. 6-29. Simple flag-clearing circuit schematic.

computer to do this, add the circuit shown in Fig. 6-29 to your interface. Be sure that you remove the wire between +5 volts and pin 1 on the SN7474. This circuit will allow a computer command, OUT 7,0, to clear the flag.

Now modify your program so that line 30 reads:

```
30   B = B+1 : OUT 7,0
```

Now run the program. Does the computer increment the count once, each time that the pulser is depressed?

It should. You may find that the count starts at one. Do you know why this might happen?

The flag may not have been cleared when the program was started. It is generally a good idea to clear flags before they are to be used, otherwise set flags may be detected, just because they were placed in the set state when the system was started.

In many applications, flags are closely associated with input ports and output ports so that the computer and I/O devices will know when information is ready. The popular 8212 or SN74412 multi-mode buffered-latch chip contains a flag flip-flop, along with latches and three-state outputs.

EXPERIMENT NO. 17
PROGRAMMABLE INTERFACE CHIPS

Purpose

The purpose of this experiment is to illustrate how general-purpose interface chips may be interfaced to the computer.

Discussion

There are many programmable interface chips that may be interfaced to microcomputer systems. The 8255 or 8255A Programmable Peripheral Interface (PPI) is an example, although there are probably over two dozen programmable chips available from various manufacturers. The steps in this experiment will serve as examples of the use of the 8255 chip For detailed uses of the 8255, we refer you to a complete book on the chip, in the "Blacksburg Continuing Education Series," *Microcomputer Interfacing with the 8255 PPI Chip* (Howard W. Sams & Co., Inc., Indianapolis, IN 46206).

Pin Configuration of the Integrated Circuit (Fig. 6-30)

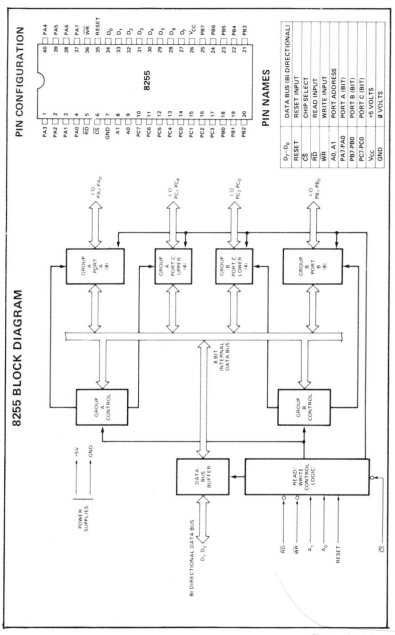

Courtesy Intel Corp.

Fig. 6-30. The 8255 Programmable Peripheral Interface (PPI) chip pin configuration and block diagram.

Step 1

Carefully examine the pin configuration of the 8255 chip presented in Fig. 6-30. You should note that there are three I/O ports and data bus connections, plus six control lines.

You will also see that the ports are labeled A, B, and C, and that port C has been divided into two groups of four lines each, lines C7-C4 and C3-C0. These are called the "upper" and "lower" portions of port C. These ports are controlled by a status register that is set by the computer to control the operation of these ports. In this experiment, only the simple I/O mode, mode zero, will be used. We refer you to the book previously referenced for additional information about the other modes of operation of the 8255.

Step 2

Note that unlike previously constructed ports, the 8255 has both a chip-select input ($\overline{CS}$) and two address inputs A1 and A0. These allow the address lines to select internal operations once the chip has been selected. You should also realize that the $\overline{IN}$ and $\overline{OUT}$ signals are used by the 8255, since $\overline{RD}$ and $\overline{WR}$ pins have been provided.

If you are not using the interface breadboard on which device addressing has been provided, you should connect address lines A0 and A1 to pins 9 and 8, respectively, using address bits A7-A2 to generate the necessary chip-select ($\overline{CS}$) signal.

If you are using the interface breadboard, you will have to make the A0 and A1 connection, but four of the device address-decoder outputs will have to be gated to provide a "chip select' signal. This is shown in Fig. 6-31. Since all input operations require the generation of an $\overline{INP\ REQ}$ signal, additional gating has been provided to perform this operation, too. The pin configurations for the SN7420 and the SN7402 gates are provided in Fig. 6-32.

Wire the circuit shown in Fig. 6-31. What addresses will generate a logic zero at the 8255 chip select input? What sequence will generate a logic zero pulse at the INP REQ "X" output?

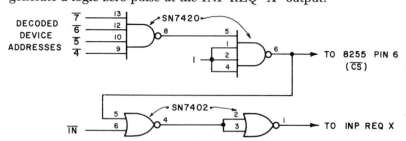

Fig. 6-31. Schematic of circuit used to generate chip-select signal for 8255 chip.

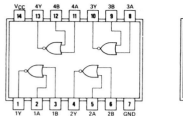 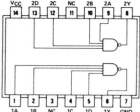

Fig. 6-32. SN7402 and SN7420 gate chip pin configurations.

The chip-select signal will be generated whenever device 7, 6, 5, or 4 is addressed. The input-request signal is generated whenever the chip is selected for an input operation. Since address bits A1 and A0 are also used, up to four devices within the 8255 chip may be controlled.

Step 3

The actual operations of the 8255 chip I/O ports are controlled by an 8-bit word that is sent to the 8255 chip by the computer. The format is shown in Fig. 6-33. Since we will only use mode zero, bits D6, D5, and D2 must always be zero. The other bits let us configure the I/O ports A, B, and C. Bit D7 must be a logic one to allow the mode information to be used by the 8255.

Using the information shown in Fig. 6-33, what control words would be required to "program" the 8255 for: a) All ports as input ports, b) port A as input, ports B and C as output, and c) all ports as output ports? Give your answers in both binary and decimal:

a)

b)

c)

You should be able to come up with the following values, a) 10011011 or 155, b) 10010000 or 144, and c) 10000000 or 129. Note that port C was not "split" or divided into sets of four lines each.

Step 4

Wire the circuit shown in Fig. 6-34. The chip-select logic circuit should be already wired on your breadboard. Pay careful attention to the power pins. They are not where you might expect to find them. The reset connection may be a jumper to ground.

In the 8255, the I/O port codes are as shown in Table 6-5. The control register is used to store the mode-control information. In

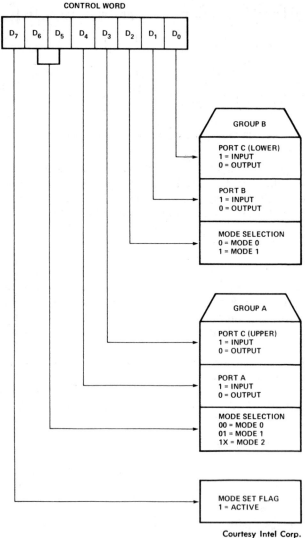

CONTROL WORD

| D_7 | D_6 | D_5 | D_4 | D_3 | D_2 | D_1 | D_0 |

GROUP B

PORT C (LOWER)
1 = INPUT
0 = OUTPUT

PORT B
1 = INPUT
0 = OUTPUT

MODE SELECTION
0 = MODE 0
1 = MODE 1

GROUP A

PORT C (UPPER)
1 = INPUT
0 = OUTPUT

PORT A
1 = INPUT
0 = OUTPUT

MODE SELECTION
00 = MODE 0
01 = MODE 1
1X = MODE 2

MODE SET FLAG
1 = ACTIVE

Courtesy Intel Corp.

Fig. 6-33. Mode-control format for 8255 PPI chip.

our computer system the addresses are device address 4 through 7, as also provided in Table 6-5.

Step 5

The control information must be sent to the 8255 chip prior to its use. The following program illustrates this:

Table 6-5. The 8255 I/O Port Addressing Codes

A1	A0	Port	Device Address
0	0	PORT A	4
0	1	PORT B	5
1	0	PORT C	6
1	1	CONTROL	7

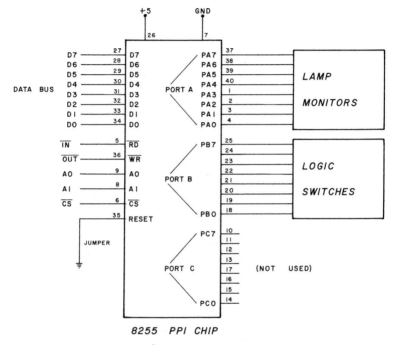

8255 PPI CHIP

Fig. 6-34. I/O configuration for 8255 chip.

```
10   OUT 7,128
20   OUT 4,0
30   END
```

This program configures all of the ports for output and then transfers the value zero to port A, or device 4 in our system. Once the chip has been programmed, it does not have to be reprogrammed unless you reset the chip, remove power or desire to change the I/O port configuration.

Write a short program that will configure the 8255 for ports A and C as output ports, with port B as an input port. Increment a count, and display it at port A.

We used the following program:

```
10   OUT 7,130
20   FOR I = 0 TO 255
30   OUT 4,I
40   NEXT I
50   GOTO 20
```

The first step was only executed once, at the start of the program, so that the 8255 chip was properly configured.

Step 6

Now write a program that will transfer the data from port B to port A.

We used the following program:

```
10   OUT 4,INP(5)
20   GOTO 10
```

We did not require another OUT 7,130 statement, since we did not wish to reconfigure the I/O ports. Using the 8255 chip in the mode zero configuration is fairly simple.

Step 7

The last characteristic of the 8255 that we wish to have you explore is the bit set/reset operation of port C. This operation allows the individual bits at port C to be independently placed in either the logic one or logic zero state.

The bit set/reset control word is shown in Fig. 6-35. It can only be used to operate on port C, and only when this port is in the output mode. Port C can, of course, still be used in the standard output mode.

The bit set/reset control word is output to the control register, *not to port C*.

Rewire your 8255 interface so that the lamp monitors are connected to port C, instead of port A. You may wish to use the following program to check for the proper operation of port C:

```
10   OUT 6,INP(5)
20   GOTO 10
```

If this program failed to operate properly, you may want to re-initialize the 8255 control register with 130, for example, OUT 7,130.

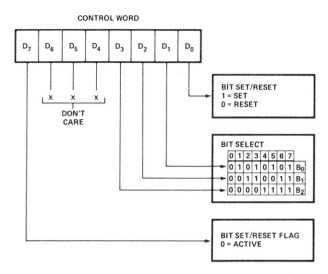

Fig. 6-35. Bit-set, bit-reset control word for port C bits in 8255 PPI chip.

Step 8

You should be able to use the information in Table 6-5, so that any bit at port C can be turned on and off. To demonstrate this, load and run the following program:

```
10   OUT 6,255
20   FOR I = 0 TO 15
30   OUT 7,I
40   FOR T = 0 TO 100: NEXT T
50   NEXT I
60   GOTO 20
```

What do you observe? In what ways has port C been used?

The lights go out and then come back on, one at a time. Port C was loaded with a value in parallel, and then the bit set/reset operations were used. Can you write a program that would turn the lights on in sequence, rather than off? Try it.

We used the following program. It was more complex than the previous "off-sequence" program. Remember to start the program with all of the lights off.

```
10  A = 1
20  FOR I = 1 TO 8
30  OUT 7,A : A = A−1
40  FOR T = 0 TO 100: NEXT T
50  OUT 7,A : A = A+3
60  FOR T = 0 TO 100: NEXT T
70  NEXT I
80  GOTO 10
```

There are many sophisticated programs that could be developed to control the 8255. In fact, the mode one and mode two operations are very complex, but they incorporate internal flags, flag checking and other features that make the 8255 a useful chip.

Our purpose here has been to have you wire and test the 8255 chip in the TRS-80 system. It is not difficult to do, and you should realize that other chips can be used in a similar manner.

If you plan to do the next experiment, you may wish to use the 8255 chip for the two input ports that are required. The power should be turned off.

EXPERIMENT NO. 18
INTERFACING AN ANALOG-TO-DIGITAL CONVERTER

Purpose

The purpose of this experiment is to show you how a simple analog-to-digital converter may be interfaced to your computer.

Discussion

This experiment is meant to introduce you to the use of A/D converters with a small computer. It is not an exhaustive study of converters or conversion techniques. Many of these, and related topics, have been covered in the "Blacksburg Continuing Education Series" book, *Microcomputer-Analog Converter Software and Hardware Interfacing* (Howard W. Sams & Co., Inc., Indianapolis, IN 46206). In this experiment, a 10-bit A/D converter will be interfaced to the computer.

The Analog Devices AD571 A/D converter has been chosen for use in this experiment because it is small, easily controlled and readily used. Two input ports are required. Similar A/D converter devices may be used.

Step 1

Two 8-bit input ports are required in this experiment. You should be able to use the schematic diagrams shown in previous experiments. If you have an 8255 chip wired to your computer, you may wish to use its B and C ports as input ports. One additional power supply is required, either −12 volts or −15 volts.

Pin Configuration of the Integrated Circuit (Fig. 6-36)

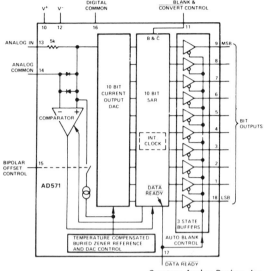

Courtesy Analog Devices, Inc.

Fig. 6-36. AD571 10-bit A/D converter chip pin configuration.

Step 2

Wire the A/D converter circuit shown in Fig. 6-37. Be careful when wiring the −12 (−15)-volt power supply. Improper wiring may damage the device.

An SN7402 NOR gate is required, so that a conversion-start pulse may be generated by the computer to tell the A/D converter when it is to start measuring the voltage present.

If you are using the previously wired 8255 chip for your input ports, be sure to ground all of the unused port inputs at port B.

Since you will also need a source of voltage to be measured, wire the potentiometer circuit shown in Fig. 6-38. *The maximum* V_{out} *should be +10 volts.*

Step 3

Connect the potentiometer V_{out} voltage line to the A/D converter ANALOG INPUT pin.

Since the AD571 can perform a complete conversion in 25 microseconds, there seems little to gain by checking the $\overline{\text{DATA READY}}$ signal. Remember, the BASIC interpreter requires at least a few milliseconds to execute a single line of your program. Therefore, once the conversion is started, the AD571 has performed the conversion before the Z-80 can even begin to interpret the next line in

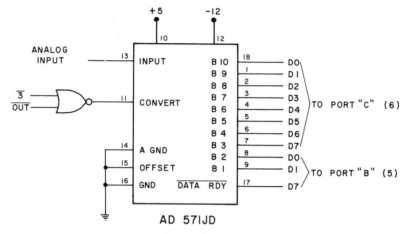

Fig. 6-37. AD571 A/D converter interface circuit schematic.

the BASIC program. If you wish to check the DATA READY signal, the following step should be used in your program:

```
XYZ   IF (128 AND INP(5)) = 1 THEN XYZ   ELSE QRS
QRS
```

In this case, the computer continues to loop through step XYZ until the flag indicates that the data are ready.

Since the AD571 generates a 10-bit data word, how would you transfer all 10 bits into the computer? Write a short test program. Remember, if you are using an 8255 chip, the chip must be reset and configured for input ports.

We used the following program:

```
10   OUT 7,155
20   OUT 3,0
40   A = INP(5)
50   B = INP(6)
60   Q = ((3 AND A)*256) + B
70   PRINT Q
80   GOTO 20
```

This program initialized the 8255 chip. Line 10 may be left out of the program if you are using standard input ports. Note the use of

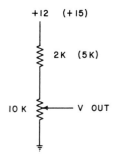

Fig. 6-38. Schematic of variable-voltage source with range of 0 to 10 volts.

the logical AND operation to mask out all except bits D1 and D2 from input port 5. Since the resulting value really represents bits D9 and D8 in the 10-bit data word, this value is multiplied by 256 before it is added to the value from the eight least significant bits.

Actually, lines 40, 50 and 60 could be rewritten as

```
40  Q = ((3 AND INP(5),*256) + INP(6)
```

leaving out lines 50 and 60. Line 30 has been left out so that a time delay could be added.

Step 4

Run the program, and vary the potentiometer. You should see the printed number change from about zero to 1023, or from 0000000000 to 1111111111 in binary. The displayed value may change by one or two, but this is an indication of noise in the system, superimposed on the analog circuitry.

Since the values are very close to the voltages, for example 1023 from the A/D converter for 10 volts, it would not be difficult to correlate the A/D converters output with an unknown voltage supplied from a temperature sensor, or other device that generated a voltage in the range of 0 to +10 volts.

Step 5

Write a program that will actually "plot" the voltage values on the tv screen used with the TRS-80. To simplify your program, use the bottom of the screen as +10 volts and the top as zero volts. You should be able to plot 128 points.

We used the following program:

```
10   OUT 7,155
20   CLS
30   FOR P = 0 TO 127
40   OUT 3,0
50   Q = ((3 AND INP(5))*256) + INP(6)
60   D = Q/22
70   SET (P,D)
80   NEXT P
90   GOTO 20
```

What happens when you run the program and adjust the potentiometer? What happens when 128 data points have been displayed?

The TRS-80 displays the points, moving them on the Y axis as the
voltage is increased or decreased. Whenever a "file" has been displayed, the screen is cleared to allow another 128 points to be displayed.

Step 6

To see how an A/D converter might be useful, wire the circuit
shown in Fig. 6-39. This is a simple R/C circuit that will charge
the capacitor at a fixed rate. When the jumper is removed from its
ground connection, the voltage across the capacitor will increase.
This increasing voltage may be measured by the TRS-80.

Connect the V_{out} signal from the R/C network to the ANALOG
INPUT pin on the AD571 A/D converter. Remove the potentiometer

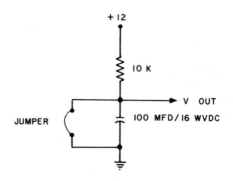

Fig. 6-39. Simple R/C charging circuit.

connection. Start the program, and just as a new data display sequence starts, remove the ground jumper. What do you observe?

We observed a characteristic R/C curve. Remember that zero volts is at the top of the screen, and +10 volts is at the bottom.

You may wish to experiment with different capacitance values during this step. The AD571 has a fairly low input resistance, so in some cases, it will load down the circuit being tested.

There are many other interesting things that may be measured (as voltages) with an A/D converter. Examples are pressure, temperature, speed, conductance, etc.

Logic Functions

In the experiments in this book, several logic functions are required. These functions are noted as lamp monitors, logic switches, and pulsers. In each case, the equivalent circuits are simple, but rather than duplicate them in each schematic diagram, block diagrams have been used. The following sections describe each of the functions that are required.

LAMP MONITORS

Lamp monitors are simply light-emitting diodes, or other on-off indicating devices that are used to indicate the state of a logical output. We have adopted the convention of logic one being the lit, or on state, and logic zero being the unlit, or off, state. The two circuits shown in Fig. A-1 may be used to construct lamp monitors. The use of red LEDs is recommended, since they are inexpensive and readily seen. You will require at least eight of the individual lamp monitors to do the experiments in this book.

LOGIC SWITCHES

Logic switches are simply switches that have been configured to provide either the logic one or the logic zero voltages to the TTL-compatible integrated circuits used in the experiments. A typical logic switch is shown in Fig. A-2. A single-pole, single-throw toggle switch or slide switch may be used. At least eight of the logic-switch circuits will be required in the experiments.

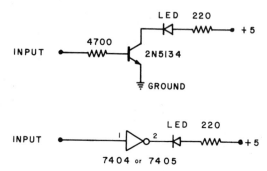

Fig. A-1. Schematics of two simple lamp-monitor circuits that may be used in experiments.

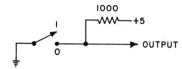

Fig. A-2. Schematic of simple logic-switch circuit that may be used to generate logic one or logic zero output.

PULSERS

The pulser circuit is used in the experiments to provide "clean" outputs that are free of the "bounce" that is normally associated with mechanical switches. Since most switches use spring-like metal contacts, the contacts will often open and close several times after the switch has been opened or closed. If such a mechanical switch is used to provide pulses to a counter, up to 30 or 40 pulses may be counted, depending on the type of switch used. Since there are many cases in which a clean logic one to logic zero, or logic zero to logic one, transition is required, a debounced switch is frequently useful. Mechanical switches are easily debounced, if they have contacts of the single-pole, double-throw form. A typical debouncing circuit is shown in Fig. A-3. In this case, two NAND gates have been used to form a flip-flop that may be set, or reset, by the switch. As shown in Fig. A-3, two outputs are available. With the switch in the position shown, the normal logic states are shown at the outputs of the two gates. When the switch is moved to the other position, the outputs of the NAND gates will switch. It is suggested that a momentary switch be used in the pulser circuits.

Lamp monitors, logic switches, and pulsers are all useful devices when breadboarding logic circuits. While the circuits shown in Figs. A-1 through A-3 are simple, you may not wish to build them yourself. Several companies produce digital breadboarding devices that incorporate lamp monitors, logic switches, and pulsers, as

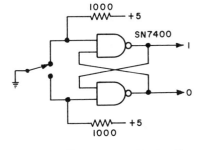

Fig. A-3. Schematic for debounced pulser in which "cross-coupled" NAND gate has been used to eliminate contact bounce.

well as other digital functions. We suggest that you write to the following companies for information about their digital-electronic breadboarding systems:

E & L Instruments, Inc.
61 First Street
Derby, CT 06418

AP Products, Inc.
Painesville, OH 44077

PACCOM
14825 NE 40th, Suite 340
Redmond, WA 98025

APPENDIX **B**

Parts Required for the Experiments

4 SN7402 Quad NOR-gate integrated circuit (IC)
2 SN7474 Dual D-type flip-flop IC
2 DM8095 or SN74365 three-state input buffer (2@ per input port)
2 SN7475 Quad latch IC
1 NE5018 Eight-bit D/A converter IC (Signetics Corporation)
1 SN7404 Hex inverter IC
1 SN74LS139 Decoder IC
1 SN73LS138 Decoder IC
2 SN74LS373 Three-state octal latch IC
1 Intel 8255 PPI IC, or equivalent
1 SN7420 Dual four-input NAND gate IC
1 AD571JD Ten-bit three-state A/D Converter IC (Analog Devices, Inc.)
1 1 0.01-μf, disc ceramic capacitor
1 4700-ohm, $\frac{1}{4}$-watt resistor
6 220-ohm, $\frac{1}{4}$-watt resistors
6 Visible LEDs (2@ red, 2@ green and 2@ yellow)
1 2000- or 5000-ohm, $\frac{1}{4}$-watt resistor (see Experiment No. 18)
1 10K, potentiometer trimmer-type
1 10K, $\frac{1}{4}$-watt resistor
1 100-μf electrolytic capacitor 16 WVDC

Besides the parts listed, you will need an assortment of SN7400, SN7408, SN7402, SN7410, SN7486, SN7430, and SN7493 integrated circuits for use in the logic-tester program in Experiment No. 15. We suggest that you read through this experiment to determine exactly which circuits you will want to test.

Other useful equipment includes: a ±12-volt power supply, for use with the A/D and D/A converter circuits, hook-up wire, an extra solderless breadboard, pulsers, lamp monitors, and logic switches.

Information about the availability of the A/D and D/A converter may be obtained directly from the respective manufacturers:

Analog Devices, Inc.
Route One Industrial Park
Norwood, MA 02062

Signetics Corporation
811 East Arques Avenue
Sunnyvale CA 94086

Z-80 Microprocessor Technical Data

The following pages contain some technical information pertaining to the Z-80 microprocessor chip. The information has been abstracted from *Mostek Microcomputer Z80 Data Book,* copyright 1978, Mostek Corporation, Carrollton, TX 75006. For more complete information, we suggest that you obtain a copy of the complete 312-page manual directly from Mostek (Publication No. 79602).

3.0 Z80-CPU PIN DESCRIPTION

The Z80–CPU is packaged in an industry standard 40 pin Dual In-Line Package. The I/O pins are shown in Figure 3.0-1 and the function of each is described below.

Z80 PIN CONFIGURATION

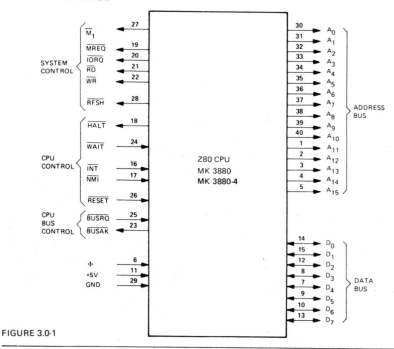

FIGURE 3.0-1

A0-A15 (Address Bus)	Tri-state output, active high. A_0-A_{15} constitute a 16-bit address bus. The address bus provides the address for memory (up to 64K bytes) data exchanges and for I/O device data exchanges. I/O addressing uses the 8 lower address bits to allow the user to directly select up to 256 input or 256 output ports. A_0 is the least significant address bit. During refresh time, the lower 7 bits contain a valid refresh address.
D0-D7 (Data Bus)	Tri-state input/output, active high. D_0-D_7 constitute an 8-bit bidirectional data bus. The data bus is used for data exchanges with memory and I/O devices.
$\overline{M_1}$ (Machine Cycle one)	Output, active low. $\overline{M_1}$ indicates that the current machine cycle is the OP code fetch cycle of an instruction execution. Note that during execution of 2-byte op-codes, $\overline{M_1}$ is generated as each op code byte is fetched. These two byte op-codes always begin with CBH, DDH, EDH, or FDH. $\overline{M_1}$ also occurs with $\overline{IORQ}$ to indicate an interrupt acknowledge cycle.
$\overline{MREQ}$ (Memory Request)	Tri-state output, active low. The memory request signal indicates that the address bus holds a valid address for a memory read or memory write operation.

$\overline{\text{IORQ}}$
(Input/Output Request)

Tri-state output, active low. The $\overline{\text{IORQ}}$ signal indicates that the lower half of the address bus holds a valid I/O address for a I/O read or write operation. An $\overline{\text{IORQ}}$ signal is also generated with an $\overline{\text{M}}_1$ signal when an interrupt is being acknowledged to indicate that an interrupt response vector can be placed on the data bus. Interrupt Acknowledge operations occur during M_1 time while I/O operations never occur during M_1 time.

$\overline{\text{RD}}$
(Memory Read)

Tri-state output, active low. $\overline{\text{RD}}$ indicates that the CPU wants to read data from memory or an I/O device. The addressed I/O device or memory should use this signal to gate data onto the CPU data bus.

$\overline{\text{WR}}$
(Memory Write)

Tri-state output, active low. $\overline{\text{WR}}$ indicates that the CPU data bus holds valid data to be stored in the addressed memory or I/O device.

$\overline{\text{RFSH}}$)
(Refresh)

Output, active low. $\overline{\text{RFSH}}$ indicates that the lower 7 bits of the address bus contain a refresh address for dynamic memories and current $\overline{\text{MREQ}}$ signal should be used to do a refresh read to all dynamic memories. A_7 is a logic zero and the upper 8 bits of the Address Bus contains the I Register.

$\overline{\text{HALT}}$
(Halt state)

Output, active low. $\overline{\text{HALT}}$ indicates that the CPU has executed a HALT software instruction and is awaiting either a non maskable or a maskable interrupt (with the mask enabled) before operation can resume. While halted, the CPU executes NOP's to maintain memory refresh activity.

$\overline{\text{WAIT}}$*
(Wait)

Input, active low. $\overline{\text{WAIT}}$ indicates to the Z80-CPU that the addressed memory or I/O devices are not ready for a data transfer. The CPU continues to enter wait states for as long as this signal is active. This signal allows memory or I/O devices of any speed to be synchronized to the CPU.

$\overline{\text{INT}}$
(Interrupt Request)

Input, active low. The Interrupt Request signal is generated by I/O devices. A request will be honored at the end of the current instruction if the internal software controlled interrupt enable flip-flop (IFF) is enabled and if the $\overline{\text{BUSRQ}}$ signal is not active. When the CPU accepts the interrupt, an acknowledge signal ($\overline{\text{IORQ}}$ during M_1 time) is sent out at the beginning of the next instruction cycle. The CPU can respond to an interrupt in three different modes that are described in detail in section 8.

$\overline{\text{NMI}}$

Input, negative edge triggered. The non maskable interrupt request line has a higher priority than $\overline{\text{INT}}$ and is always recognized at the end of the current instruction, independent of the status of the interrupt enable flip-flop. $\overline{\text{NMI}}$ automatically forces the Z80-CPU to restart to location 0066_H. The program counter is automatically saved in the external stack so that the user can return to the program that was interrupted. Note that continuous WAIT cycles can prevent the current instruction from ending, and that a $\overline{\text{BUSRQ}}$ will override a $\overline{\text{NMI}}$.

RESET   Input, active low. $\overline{\text{RESET}}$ forces the program counter to zero and
                         initializes the CPU. The CPU initialization includes:

                         1) Disable the interrupt enable flip-flop
                         2) Set Register I = 00$_H$
                         3) Set Register R = 00$_H$
                         4) Set Interrupt Mode 0

                         During reset time, the address bus and data bus go to a high
                         impedance state and all control output signals go to the inactive
                         state. No refresh occurs.

$\overline{\text{BUSRQ}}$ Input, active low. The bus request signal is used to request the
(Bus Request)   CPU address bus, data bus and tri-state output control signals to
                         go to a high impedance state so that other devices can control
                         these buses. When $\overline{\text{BUSRQ}}$ is activated, the CPU will set these
                         buses to a high impedance state as soon as the current CPU
                         machine cycle is terminated.

$\overline{\text{BUSAK}}$*   Output, active low. Bus acknowledge is used to indicate to the
(Bus Acknowledge)   requesting device that the CPU address bus, data bus and tri-
                         state control bus signals have been set to their high impedance
                         state and the external device can now control these signals.

                         Single phase system clock.

*While the Z80-CPU is in either a $\overline{\text{WAIT}}$ state or a Bus Acknowledge condition, Dynamic Memory Refresh
will not occur.

4.0 CPU TIMING

The Z80-CPU executes instructions by stepping through a very precise set of a few basic operations. These include:

Memory read or write

I/O device read or write

Interrupt acknowledge

All instructions are merely a series of these basic operations. Each of these basic operations can take from three to six clock periods to complete or they can be lengthened to synchronize the CPU to the speed of external devices. The basic clock periods are referred to as T states and the basic operations are referred to as M (for machine) cycles. Figure 4.0-0 illustrates how a typical instruction will be merely a series of specific M and T cycles. Notice that this instruction consists of three machine cycles (M1, M2 and M3). The first machine cycle of any instruction is a fetch cycle which is four, five or six T states long (unless lengthened by the wait signal which will be fully described in the next section). The fetch cycle (M1) is used to fetch the OP code of the next instruction to be executed. Subsequent machine cycles move data between the CPU and memory or I/O devices and they may have anywhere from three to five T cycles (again they may be lengthened by wait states to synchronize the external devices to the CPU). The following paragraphs describe the timing which occurs within any of the basic machine cycles. In section 7, the exact timing for each instruction is specified.

BASIC CPU TIMING EXAMPLE

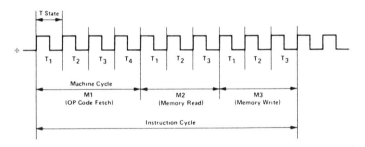

FIGURE 4.0-0

All CPU timing can be broken down into a few very simple timing diagrams as shown in Figure 4.0-1 through 4.0-7. These diagrams show the following basic operations with and without wait states (wait states are added to synchronize the CPU to slow memory or I/O devices).

        4.0-1. Instruction OP code fetch (M1 cycle)

        4.0-2. Memory data read or write cycles

        4.0-3. I/O read or write cycles

        4.0-4. Bus Request/Acknowledge Cycle

        4.0-5. Interrupt Request/Acknowledge Cycle

        4.0-6. Non maskable Interrupt Request/Acknowledge Cycle

        4.0-7. Exit from a HALT instruction

INSTRUCTION FETCH

Figure 4.0-1 shows the timing during an M1 cycle (OP code fetch). Notice that the PC is placed on the address bus at the beginning of the M1 cycle. One half clock time later the $\overline{\text{MREQ}}$ signal goes active. At this time the address to the memory has had time to stabilize so that the falling edge of $\overline{\text{MREQ}}$ can be used directly as a chip enable clock to dynamic memories. The $\overline{\text{RD}}$ line also goes active to indicate that the memory read data should be enabled onto the CPU data bus. The CPU samples the data from the memory on the data bus with the rising edge of the clock of state T3 and this same edge is used by the CPU to turn off the $\overline{\text{RD}}$ and $\overline{\text{MREQ}}$ signals. Thus the data has already been sampled by the CPU before the $\overline{\text{RD}}$ signal becomes inactive. Clock state T3 and T4 of a fetch cycle are used to refresh dynamic memories. (The CPU uses this time to decode and execute the fetched instruction so that no other operation could be performed at this time). During T3 and T4 the lower 7 bits of the address bus contain a memory refresh address and the $\overline{\text{RFSH}}$ signal becomes active to indicate that a refresh read of all dynamic memories should be accomplished. Notice that a $\overline{\text{RD}}$ signal is not generated during refresh time to prevent data from different memory segments from being gated onto the data bus. The $\overline{\text{MREQ}}$ signal during refresh time should be used to perform a refresh read of all memory elements. The refresh signal can not be used by itself since the refresh address is only guaranteed to be stable during $\overline{\text{MREQ}}$ time.

INSTRUCTION OP CODE FETCH

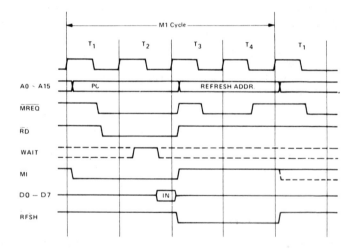

FIGURE 4.0-1

Figure 4.0-1A illustrates how the fetch cycle is delayed if the memory activates the $\overline{\text{WAIT}}$ line. During T2 and every subsequent Tw, the CPU samples the $\overline{\text{WAIT}}$ line with the falling edge of Φ. If the $\overline{\text{WAIT}}$ line is active at this time, another wait state will be entered during the following cycle. Using this technique the read cycle can be lengthened to match the access time of any type of memory device.

INSTRUCTION OP CODE FETCH WITH WAIT STATES

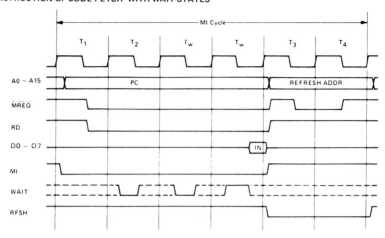

FIGURE 4.0-1A

MEMORY READ OR WRITE

Figure 4.0-2 illustrates the timing of memory read or write cycles other than an OP code fetch (M1 cycle). These cycles are generally three clock periods long unless wait states are requested by the memory via the $\overline{WAIT}$ signal. The $\overline{MREQ}$ signal and the $\overline{RD}$ signal are used the same as in the fetch cycle. In the case of a memory write cycle, the $\overline{MREQ}$ also becomes active when the address bus is stable so that it can be used directly as a chip enable for dynamic memories. The $\overline{WR}$ line is active when data on the data bus is stable so that it can be used directly as a R/W pulse to virtually any type of semiconductor memory. Furthermore the $\overline{WR}$ signal goes inactive one half T state before the address and data bus contents are changed so that the overlap requirements for virtually any type of semiconductor memory type will be met.

MEMORY READ OR WRITE CYCLES

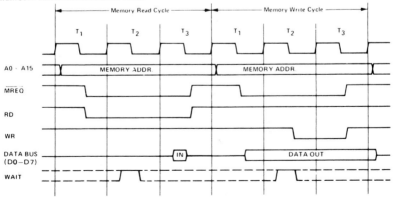

FIGURE 4.0-2

Figure 4.0-2A illustrates how a $\overline{WAIT}$ request signal will lengthen any memory read or write operation. This operation is identical to that previously described for a fetch cycle. Notice in this figure that a separate read and a separate write cycle are shown in the same figure although read and write cycles can never occur simultaneously.

MEMORY READ OR WRITE CYCLES WITH WAIT STATES

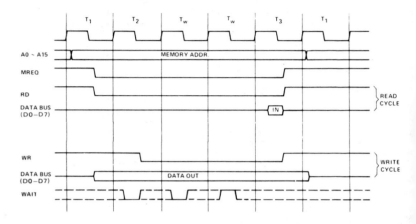

FIGURE 4.0-2A

INPUT OR OUTPUT CYCLES

Figure 4.0-3 illustrates an I/O read or I/O write operation. Notice that during I/O operations a single wait state is automatically inserted. The reason for this is that during I/O operations, the time from when the $\overline{IORQ}$ signal goes active until the CPU must sample the $\overline{WAIT}$ line is very short and without this extra state sufficient time does not exist for an I/O port to decode its address and activate the $\overline{WAIT}$ line if a wait is required. Also, without this wait state it is difficult to design MOS I/O devices that can operate at full CPU speed. During this wait state time the $\overline{WAIT}$ request signal is sampled. During a read I/O operation, the $\overline{RD}$ line is used to enable the addressed port onto the data bus just as in the case of a memory read. For I/O write operations, the $\overline{WR}$ line is used as a clock to the I/O port, again with sufficient overlap timing automatically provided so that the rising edge may be used as a data clock.

Figure 4.0-3A illustrates how additional wait states may be added with the $\overline{WAIT}$ line. The operation is identical to that previously described.

BUS REQUEST/ACKNOWLEDGE CYCLE

Figure 4.0-4 illustrates the timing for a Bus Request/Acknowledge cycle. The $\overline{BUSRQ}$ signal is sampled by the CPU with the rising edge of the last clock period of any machine cycle. If the $\overline{BUSRQ}$ signal is active, the CPU will set its address, data and tri-state control signals to the high impedance state with the rising edge of the next clock pulse. At that time any external device can control the buses to transfer data between memory and I/O devices. (This is generally known as Direct Memory Access [DMA] using cycle stealing). The maximum time for the CPU to respond to a bus request is the length of a machine cycle and the external controller can maintain control of the bus for as many clock cycles as is desired. Note, however, that if very long DMA cycles are used, and dynamic memories are being used, the external controller must also perform the refresh function. This situation only occurs if very large blocks of data are transferred under DMA control. Also note that during a bus request cycle, the CPU cannot be interrupted by either a $\overline{NMI}$ or an $\overline{INT}$ signal.

INPUT OR OUTPUT CYCLES

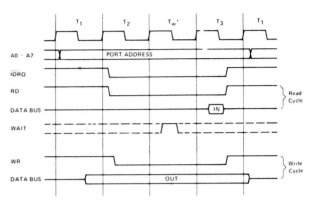

FIGURE 4.0-3

INPUT OR OUTPUT CYCLES WITH WAIT STATES

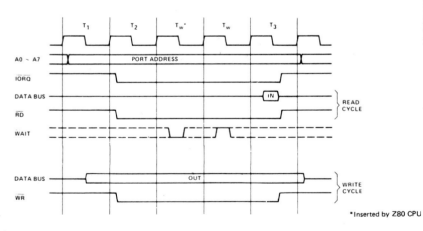

FIGURE 4.0-3A

177

BUS REQUEST/ACKNOWLEDGE CYCLE

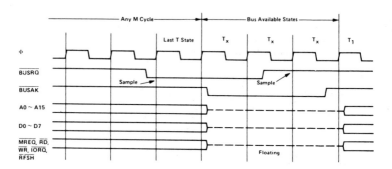

FIGURE 4.0-4

INTERRUPT REQUEST/ ACKNOWLEDGE CYCLE

Figure 4.0-5 illustrates the timing associated with an interrupt cycle. The interrupt signal ($\overline{INT}$) is sampled by the CPU with the rising edge of the last clock at the end of any instruction. The signal will not be accepted if the internal CPU software controlled interrupt enable flip-flop is not set or if the $\overline{BUSRQ}$ signal is active. When the signal is accepted a special M1 cycle is generated. During this special M1 cycle the $\overline{IORQ}$ signal becomes active (instead of the normal $\overline{MREQ}$) to indicate that the interrupting device can place an 8-bit vector on the data bus. Notice that two wait states are automatically added to this cycle. These states are added so that a ripple priority interrupt scheme can be easily implemented. The two wait states allow sufficient time for the ripple signals to stablilize and identify which I/O device must insert the response vector. Refer to section 8.0 for details on how the interrupt response vector is utilized by the CPU.

INTERRUPT REQUEST/ACKNOWLEDGE CYCLE

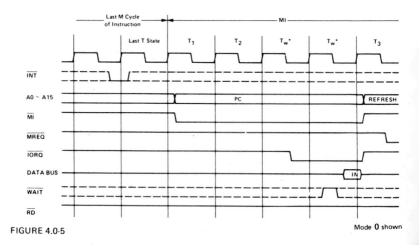

FIGURE 4.0-5

Mode 0 shown

Figure 4.0-5A illustrates how additional wait states can be added to the interrupt response cycle. Again the operation is identical to that previously described.

INTERRUPT REQUEST/ACKNOWLEDGE WITH WAIT STATES

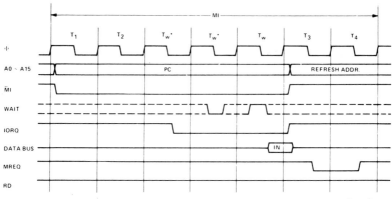

Mode 0 shown

FIGURE 4.0-5A

NON MASKABLE INTERRUPT RESPONSE

Figure 4.0-6 illustrates the request/acknowledge cycle for the non-maskable interrupt. A pulse on the $\overline{\text{NMI}}$ input sets an internal NMI latch which is tested by the CPU at the end of every instruction. This NMI latch is sampled at the same time as the interrupt line, but this line has priority over the normal interrupt and it can not be disabled under software control. Its usual function is to provide immediate response to important signals such as an impending power failure. The CPU response to a non maskable interrupt is similar to a normal memory read operation. The only difference being that the content of the data bus is ignored while the processor automatically stores the PC in the external stack and jumps to location 0066_H. The service routine for the non maskable interrupt must begin at this location if this interrupt is used.

HALT EXIT

Whenever a software halt instruction is executed the CPU begins executing NOP's until an interrupt is received (either a non-maskable or a maskable interrupt while the interrupt flip flop is enabled). The two interrupt lines are sampled with the rising clock edge during each T4 state as shown in Figure 4.0-7. If a non-maskable interrupt has been received or a maskable interrupt has been received and the interrupt enable flip-flop is set, then the halt state will be exited on the next rising clock edge. The following cycle will then be an interrupt acknowledge cycle corresponding to the type of interrupt that was received. If both are received at this time, then the non maskable one will be acknowledged since it was highest priority. The purpose of executing NOP instructions while in the halt state is to keep the memory refresh signals active. Each cycle in the halt state is a normal M1 (fetch) cycle except that the data received from the memory is ignored and a NOP instruction is forced internally to the CPU. The halt acknowledge signal is active during this time to indicate that the processor is in the halt state.

NON MASKABLE INTERRUPT REQUEST OPERATION

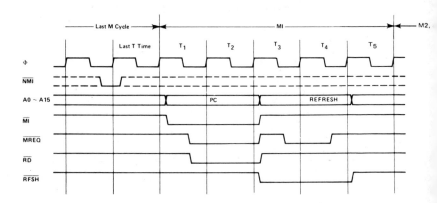

*M2 and M3 are stack write op

FIGURE 4.0-6

HALT EXIT

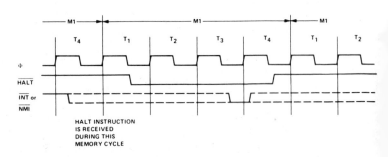

HALT INSTRUCTION
IS RECEIVED
DURING THIS
MEMORY CYCLE

FIGURE 4.0-7

TRS-80 Interface
Breadboard Parts

Parts required for the construction of the TRS-80 Interface Breadboard:

IC 1 & 7	16-pin resistor network, eight independent 1000-ohm resistors
IC 2 & 6	8-position DIP switch (on-off)
IC 3, 4, & 5	SN74LS85 Quad comparator IC (DO NOT SUBSTITUTE SN74L85)
IC 8	SN74LS20 Dual four-input NAND gate IC
IC 9	SN74365 or DM8095 three-state buffer
IC 10 & 11	8216 Noninverting bus buffer, Intel or equivalent
IC 12	SN74154 decoder IC
IC 13	SN7404 inverter IC
IC 14	SN74123 or SN74LS123 dual monostable IC
IC 15	LM319N Dual comparator (14-pin package)
IC 16, 17, 18, & 20	High-quality 16-pin IC sockets, Augat 516-AG-10D, or equivalent
IC 19	High-quality 8-pin IC socket, Augat 508-AG-10D, or equivalent
D1 - D4	1N4001 50 PIV, 1-ampere diodes*
D5	Yellow LED
D6	Red LED
D7	Green LED
D8 & D9	1N4148 or 1N4154, small-signal diodes
R1 & R8	1000-ohm, ¼-watt resistor

R2 & R3	220-ohm, $\frac{1}{4}$-watt resistor
R4 & R5	47K, $\frac{1}{4}$-watt resistor
R6	3900-ohm, $\frac{1}{4}$-watt resistor
R7	2200-ohm, $\frac{1}{4}$-watt resistor
C1	2200-μf, 16 WVDC electrolytic capacitor (axial)*
C2, 4 & 5	0.1-μf disc ceramic, 50-volt capacitors
C3 & C6	1-μf, 35 WVDC tantalum electrolytic capacitors
C7 & C8	3.3 μf, 50 WVDC electrolytic capacitors (axial)
VR	LM309K 5-volt, 1-amp voltage regulator*
P1	Molex right-angle 6-pin connector (PN 09-75-1061) optional
	Requires 1@ mating female housing (PN09-50-7061) and 6@ connector pins (PN 08-50-0106 or 08-50-0108)
P2	4-pin right-angle jumper header, AP Products 923875R, or equivalent
T1	12.6 VAC transformer 1 amp
Misc.	11 16-pin IC sockets
	3 14-pin IC sockets
	1 24-pin IC socket
	Cable assembly: 40-pin header on one end, with a 40-pin card edge connector on the other, facing the same direction
	Solderless breadboard socket, SK-10, Superstrip, or equivalent, 4@ 4-40 × $\frac{5}{8}$ flat-head mach. screws, 4@ #4 internal-tooth lock washers, 4@ #4 hex nuts.
	Heat sink for VR, 2@ 4-40 × $\frac{1}{2}$ mach. screws, 2@ #4 internal-tooth lockwashers, 2@ #4 hex nuts, mica insulator, thermal grease (optional).
	Power cord

The parts marked with "*" are not required if an external +5-volt power supply will be used to power the system.

A printed-circuit board is available from

Techniques, Inc.
235 Jackson St.
Englewood, NJ 07631

A complete package, containing a case, power supply, etc., is available from

E & L Instruments, Inc.
61 First Street
Derby, CT 06418

203 735 8774

Printed-Circuit
Board Artwork

This appendix contains artwork that may be used to make a printed-circuit board of the TRS-80 Interfacing Breadboard. Since the artwork has been reduced, it must be enlarged before it can be used. We recommend that you have a print shop make a high-contrast film negative, or positive, depending on the process that you will use. The long thick black line in each of the three diagrams should be enlarged so that it is four (4) inches long. The process-camera operator should be able to correct the enlarging process so that the resulting film is the right size for the printed-circuit board. You may not choose to use the parts overlay, but it has been provided as a guide to the placement of the various parts.

A completely etched, double-sided printed-circuit board is available from

Techniques, Inc.
235 Jackson Street
Englewood, NJ 07631

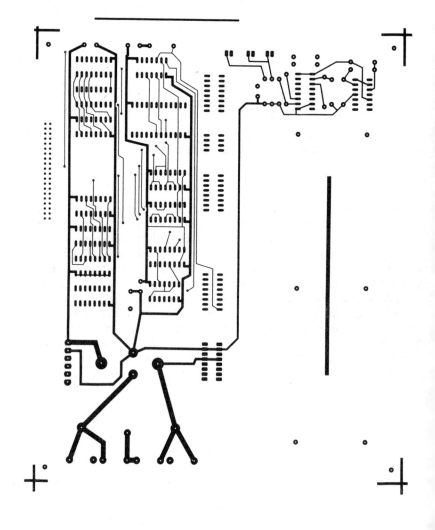

Fig. E-1. Printed-circuit board artwork for component side of interface breadboard (right reading).

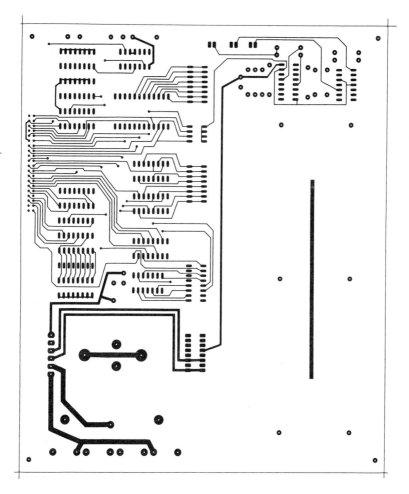

GROUND 8, 31, 39, 29

Fig. E-2. Printed-circuit board artwork for solder side of interface breadboard (reverse reading).

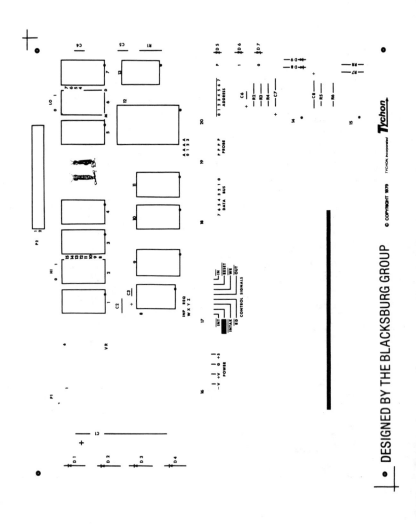

Fig. E-3. Nomenclature overlay for interface breadboard (right reading).

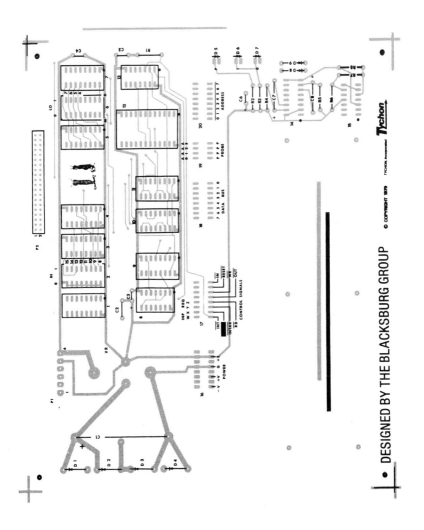

Fig. E-4. Component nomenclature overlay superimposed on component-side foil pattern, may be used as parts placement guide.

Index

A

Absolute decoding, 37-38
Address
  bus, 15
  decoder, 73
    use of, 88-92
  decoding, using gates for, 29-34
  detecting gate, 34
AD571 converter, 157-158
Analog-to-digital converter, interfacing, 156-161
Assembly Language and BASIC, 24-25

B

"Bar" over, 13
BASIC interpreter program, 11
BCD codes, 130-135
Bidirectional, 10
Binary
  and decimal numbering, 25-26
  codes, 130-135
Breadboard
  basic, 69-81
  construction, 79-81
Breadboarding with TRS-80, 69-81
Bus
  address, 15
  buffers, 75-76
  control, 15
  data, 15
"Bus conflict," 78
byte, 9

C

Central processing unit (CPU), 9
$\overline{\text{CLEAR}}$, 66
Codes
  bcd, 130-135
  binary, 130-135
Comparator and decoder used for device selections, 45
Comparing, 29
Complex flags, 64-65
Control
  bus, 15
  circuitry, 76-79
Converter, digital-to-analog, 118-123

D

Data
  bus, 15
  logging and display, 114-118
  transfer and control, 23-24
Decimal, and binary numbering, 25-26
Decisions, flags and, 61-68
Decoding, 29
Device
  address-decoder circuits, 123-130
  addressing, 28-45
  and memory decoders, 72-75
  interfacing, I/O, 47-60
  -select pulse, 34
    using, 92-95
$\overline{\text{DEVICE ADDRESS}}$, 31
Devices, some I/O, 22

Digital-to-analog converter, 118-123

E

8255 PPI chip, 149, 150, 152, 153
Experiments
  introduction to, 83-85
  TRS-80 interfacing, 83-161

F

Field-programmed memory, 12
Flag(s), 61-68
  circuits, 65-67, 145-148
  -detecting software, 63-64
Function pulse, 34

G

Gate
  address detecting, 34
  NOR, 34
  on, 34
Gating, 28-29
  circuit, programmable, 31-32
General-purpose
  I/O commands, 17-19
  memory commands, 19-20

I

IC-16 (socket), 71
IN signal, 14-15, 76-77
Input/Output
  (I/O) devices, 14-15
  pins, 11
Input part(s), 18, 52-58
  applications, 101-108
  constructing, 96-99
  multibyte, 99-101
  two-bit, 58
INTAK signal, 76-77
Interface chips, programmable, 148-156
Interfacing
  analog-to-digital converter, 156-161
  experiments, TRS-80, 83-161
  TRS-80, 27-45
Interpretation software, 25
Interrupts, 67-68
Inverter, 29
I/O
  commands, 15-17
  device
    address decoding, 27-28

I/O—cont
  device
    interfacing, 47-60
    synchronization, 61-62
I/OR signal, 14
I/OW signal, 14

L

Lamp monitors, 163-164
Large decoders, 38-43
Latch, 47-52
Least significant bit (LSB), 10
Level II BASIC, 11
Logic
  -device tester, 139-145
  functions, 163-166
  probe, 71-72
    use of, 85-88
  switches, 163-164
Logical operations and flags, 62-63

M

Mask, 63
Masked-programmed memory, 12
Memory, 10-14
  addressing, 28
  chips, 12
  -mapped I/O, 58-60
MEMR signal, 13
MEMW signal, 13
Monitors, lamp, 163-164
Most significant bit (MSB), 10
Multibyte input ports, 99-101
Multiple flags, 67

N

Nonabsolute device addressing, 37-38
NOR and OR gates, 34
NOR-gate control circuit, 133
Numbering, binary and decimal, 25-26

O

Octal latch, 51
OUT signal, 14-15, 76-77
Output port(s), 18, 47-52, 130-135
  constructing, 108-112
Output-port and input-port interactions, 112-114
Output-ports traffic-light controller, 135-139

P

Parts
  required for experiments, 167-168
  TRS-80 breadboard interface, 181
PEEK
  and POKE command timing relationships, 24
  instructions, 19-23
Pins, input/output, 11
POKE instructions, 19-23
Port(s), 18
  input, 18
  output, 18
Positions, 10
Power supply, 69-71
Printed-circuit board artwork, 183-187
Probe, logic, 71-72
Processor, Z-80, 9-26
Programmable
  gating circuit, 31-32
  interface chips, 148-156
Pulsers, 164-165

Q

Q outputs, 49

R

Random-access memory (RAM), 13
R/C charging circuit, 160
RD* notations, 13
$\overline{RD}$ signal, 76-77
Read-Only memory (ROM), 11
READ ($\overline{RD}$) control signal, 13
Read/Write (R/W) memory, 11
RESET signal, 76-77

S

SK-10 socket, 81
SN7400 NAND-gate chips, 140-141
SN7402 gate chip, 151
SN7420 gate chip, 151
SN7454 latch, 48-49
SN7474 flip-flop chip, 146
SN7485 comparator, 44
SN7493 4-bit counter, 144
SN7585 comparator chip, 43
SN74125 bus buffer chip, 53
SN74154 decoder, 40, 41-42
SN74155 decoder, 41

SN74175 latch, 48-50
SN74365 chip, 56, 96
  (DM8095) three-state bus driver chip, 55
SN74LS138 decoder, 39, 123-125, 128
SN74LS139, 123-124, 129
SN74LS244 three-state bus driver chip, 55, 57
SN74LS373 latch, 48-49, 51, 130-131
Software
  commands and interface circuits, 20-22
  I/O control instructions, 15-26
Status flag(s), 61
"Super Strip," 81
Switches, logic, 163-164
Synchronization, I/O device, 61-62

T

Tester, logic-device, 139-145
Three-state bus, 53-56
Traffic-light controller, output-ports, 135-139
TRS-80 interfacing, 27-45
  breadboard ports, 181-182
  experiments, 83-161
Two-bit input ports, 58
Two-line to four-line decoder, 36

U

Ultraviolet light, 12
Using
  comparators, 43-45
  decoders, 35-38

V

Value, 10
Volatile, 12

W

WR* notations, 13
$\overline{WR}$ signal, 76-77
WRITE ($\overline{WR}$) control signal, 13

Z

Z-80 microprocessor
  chip pin configurations, 11
  technical data, 169-179
Z-80 processor, 9-26

TO THE READER

This book is one of an expanding series of books that will cover the field of basic electronics and digital electronics from basic gates and flip-flops through microcomputers and digital telecommunications. We are attempting to develop a mailing list of individuals who would like to receive information on the series. We would be delighted to add your name to it if you would fill in the information below and mail this sheet to us. Thanks.

1. I have the following books:

_____

_____

_____

_____

_____

_____

_____

_____

_____

_____

_____

_____

2. My occupation is: ☐ student   ☐ teacher, instructor   ☐ hobbyist

   ☐ housewife   ☐ scientist, engineer, doctor, etc.   ☐ businessman

   ☐ Other: _____

Name (print): _____

Address _____

City _____   State _____

Zip Code _____

Mail to:

   Books
   P.O. Box 715
   Blacksburg, Virginia 24060